FINDING LIGHT IN UNEXPECTED PLACES

An Anthology of Surprises
Volume 1

Edited by Maria Jerinic & Erik Pihel

Palamedes

San Francisco

Palamedes Publishing
www.palamedes.pub
San Francisco

Cover by Lorna Rae Daniel
www.lornarae.co.za

ISBN 978-0-9996930-0-1
LCCN 2019940270

Also available in ebook:
Kindle d19e516c-23ba-484e-9da6-847a7f4c123e
EPUB a5d22e7a-8c02-4ab6-818d-716939ff15e1
www.palamedes.pub/books/finding-light

www.facebook.com/PalamedesPub
www.twitter.com/PalamedesPub
www.instagram.com/PalamedesPub

Candles in the Snow

Hidden Light in Famous Events

The Wonder of the Ordinary

Untethered

Introduction

The illusion of inner darkness is that it's permanent, that it will never end. Like a virtual-reality headset, the mind creates its own all-encompassing reality that blocks out everything else. A dark simulation is especially convincing and contrary evidence can seem irrelevant. To someone living inside such a headset, external stimuli—a sunrise, a walk through the woods, a phone call from a friend—might have no effect.

The mind's ability to filter, distort, or even hide reality should give us all pause. It's not always trustworthy. Our "manacles," to use William Blake's phrase, are "mind-forg'd" in that our thoughts create an inner prison. We forget that we've done this to ourselves and the manacles appear externally imposed and real.

In extended cases, this mind state can lead to despair. Old escape valves no longer work and familiar signposts turn into prison bars. The Christian mystic Saint John of the Cross called such a mind state "the dark night of the soul," a sense that the current structures of one's life are no longer reliable. This can push a soul to despair, but can also lead to dropping our chains. A deeper sense of calmness might arise, an inner awareness that does not rely on transient structures. And this is the spiritual power of the dark night: to shift us out of ourselves to a deeper sense of being and to find that joy still exists.

The spiritual power of literature, the written word, can

provide assistance along the way. The psychologist Jonathan Haidt addresses both our minds' tendency to wrestle in darkness and our need for words to help us see the light. In *The Happiness Hypothesis*, Haidt explores, via ancient texts, why our minds "have a bias toward seeing threats and engaging in useless worry." Ancient wisdom and contemporary science connect: our problem is not a new one. Words provide one path through the struggle because reading reminds us we are not alone in our darkness and relief is possible. The words of others might encourage us to break the stranglehold of fear and worry that humans seem predisposed to experience. There is also the promise posed by writing. To write is to reflect, and we might process our own experiences through the lens of writers who have come before us and who work today.

This anthology celebrates this path. The writers of these essays focus on moments when the mind's patterns abruptly stop, revealing a reservoir of inner resources. A creative life-force unexpectedly bursts forth through the fissures. Sometimes this shift arises from soul-splitting tragedy: terrorist attacks, earthquakes, and fires, which break apart ordered routines. When the outside world no longer gives us what we expect or need, sometimes an inner wellspring streams forth. The wisdom beneath chaos can be revealed anywhere, at any time because it's always there, no matter how buried. "In a dark time," the poet Theodore Roethke wrote, "the eye begins to see." When the usual distractions disappear, we come to know a deeper part of ourselves. Life is unpredictable and sometimes the only way to see that is when the structures of our lives are ripped away.

There are also times when life bombards us with smaller tragedies, the daily drip of worry's water faucet that wears down our ability to see the light. This collection examines those moments too, moments when a routine repeated one too many times reveals the limits of what we consider "real life," and we must find a way to revitalize our sense of awe and appreciation for the world. Less dramatic than revelations from tragic interruptions, beauty and the hope it inspires can appear in many places and shapes if we learn to *see*.

We expect inspiration in sunsets, blooming flowers, and mountain-top views. And in turn we've come to *not* expect it elsewhere: in the tragic or mundane. This essay collection challenges this categorization of wonder, light, and beauty. These essays find wonder in squawking gulls, beauty in aging bodies, and traces of camaraderie in the way a friend signs his name. Awe arises in the doldrums of an evening commute, when an egret unexpectedly appears on the side of the highway, made almost invisible by the rush of traffic.

It's our hope that reading these essays will fill you with wonder. Perhaps reading these essays will inspire you to write about your own moments of light and to share your words with others. Wherever you are, whatever thoughts might be racing through your mind, whatever storm clouds might be moving across the geopolitical landscape, light and beauty are available. They might be just around the corner.

Erik Pihel and Maria Jerinic
in a dark time with flashes of light
2019

Candles in the Snow

Snow and Bones

Kristin Procter

C hromosomes from generations of snow-worn women swirled inside me like a Canadian blizzard. My bones formed in winter's womb. When I finally emerged to February's bite, the earth cradled me in its frosty arms.

Growing up in Southern Ontario, spring smelled like earthworms and thawing dirt. Summers buzzed with mosquitoes and asphalt mirages. Autumn's scarlet fireworks reflected in ice-covered puddles. But it was winter's arrival that always stung my eyes and stole my breath.

The seasons shifted below consciousness. I didn't appreciate their rhythm until I traded them for a less fluctuating clime. The people of my new city, Canberra, raved that it was one of the few places in Australia that *truly* experienced the seasons. I watched and waited. Summer weeks appeared to evaporate unharnessed by the rhythm of falling leaves or accumulating frost. Weather fluctuated from hot and dry to slightly more or less hot and dry. It was years before I perceived the subtleties of seasons that the locals took such pride in—a slight shift in the thickness of air or the texture of grass. Eventually, my blood thinned and my bones softened—I acclimated. How quickly my eyes forgot lash-frozen tears. A few years later, when I birthed a baby to the thirsty red dust, he was the first child for generations unbitten by winter's kiss.

§

"'Dis? 'dat?" my son Gavin asked, pointing as he crawled through the backyard.

"This is dirt. That's a cockatoo," I responded.

As his words fell into sentences, he once asked about "puffs up there." I searched the sky, expecting to find a helicopter or hot air balloon.

"Bud, I don't see anything," I offered, confused.

"Mummy, the fluffy bits. There," he insisted, pointing a pudgy finger.

Gavin, however, accustomed to a spotless sky, was captivated by the mere existence of clouds. Born to a different climate, I wondered if his body could miss weather it had never known.

Once, when he was a toddler, it rained like it hadn't for decades. I pulled out a rubber rain suit, salvaged from a bag of hand-me-downs. Covered head to toe, he waddled along for a while before he froze, entranced by the patter of droplets. Despite my encouragement to move, he remained immobile. Arms raised in adulation, he breathed in the scent of wet eucalypts, and felt the slipperiness of each raindrop on his fingers. Statue-still he affixed the moisture to his drought-born bones.

§

When Gavin turned four, our family moved from Australia to Boston. In preparing Gavin, we talked about trick-or-treating, and baseball. He shrugged. We read about a wolf sanctuary, but he teared up thinking of leaving the kangaroos and kookaburras he loved. Finally, tales of tobogganing piqued his interest, so we promised a New England winter full of snow.

After the first few weeks of extreme-parenting-through-jet-lag, I stumbled outdoors to breathe in September. One line of trees shimmered in the middle of their autumnal transformation, while a greener clump clung to their warm-weather attire. Summer had stretched her fingers into fall, and fall took her time passing the baton to winter.

One morning near Halloween, steam rose off the grass, as if each blade were straining to breathe. Gavin and I ran outside to explore this almost-snow. Gavin tried unsuccessfully to scrape enough frost together for a snowball, but by breakfast time the courtyard returned to green, as if we had only imagined winter's visit.

November unfolded as it had in Canada—the wind undressing the trees and blanketing the yard in leaves. December brought crafts: snow globes and snow dough. The only flakes were those we cut from paper. We remained unrelenting in our optimism that we would wake one day to find our yard transformed into a snow-covered New England Christmas Card.

Christmas came, but it didn't snow. New Year's arrived.

Still no snow.

On January 19th, I divined the fair-weather forecast by the depth of Gavin's sigh at the window. His icy toes and pleas for breakfast pried me from the cocoon of blankets. I reached for the box of cereal, refusing Gavin's request for brownies for breakfast, when I noticed the first fluttering white flake.

"Look, snow!" I squealed and pointed out the glass doors behind Gavin.

My ribs hummed with childhood memories, melting flakes on my tongue, eating syrup-snow, sliding along my belly like an otter. I could hear the winter whisper to my child, *your bones are made of snow.*

Gavin craned his neck desperate for a glimpse. Unable to see, he squirmed half-way off the iron stool, then lost his foothold. Before I could admonish him, he had tumbled to the floor, a tangle of iron and flesh.

"Don't move," I insisted, as I ran around the breakfast bar.

He wriggled and wailed with howls that seared my skin. He unknotted himself from the web of metal, and I pressed my lips into his forehead.

"Take me to a doctor right away!" he cried.

His dad lifted him off the floor and I ran my hands over his right thigh. Feeling a non-descript bump, I grabbed a bag of frozen peas to assuage the tears. Zippered snugly in his one-piece pajama suit with dinosaurs riding bicycles, he pointed towards his leg.

"I need a doctor. Right now!" His color shifted from pink to gray.

"I'm going to be late for work," Simon mumbled, worried about his new job.

"I think we have to take him to the hospital," I said, then added, "but what are the chances he broke the biggest bone in his body?"

Flakes clumped together in clusters that stuck to my eyelashes. The wind groaned. The brisk air brought my exhalations to life and the evergreens swayed with worried expressions. I wanted to reassure the trees and the wind that everything was going to be okay. Everything was going to be okay.

As we drove, I searched outside for just the right sight to distract him—perhaps a cardinal or a forgotten Christmas lights. I needed words to fill the eerie quiet in a car usually a cacophony of dinosaur tunes and questions. Remembering his delight in simple snowflakes, I turned to show Gavin the wet splotches on his windows as the delicate ice crystals melted. His fingers curled into fists and shallow breaths rasped through his pale lips. His eyes glazed as he sunk beyond my small talk and snowflakes.

At the hospital, Gavin and I were seen by intake staff, who asked for insurance cards and primary care providers and whether we were part of their network. Despite speaking English, I felt lost in this foreign language. Gavin writhed in my arms, asking for help, while I filled out flurries of paperwork. At most this took half an hour, but caught in the yowls of his pain, I felt trapped by infinite sheets of ice.

Eventually we were told that Gavin broke the bone in his thigh (a more common occurrence in children than I had thought). A nurse, whose words drizzled from her mouth like molasses, asked Gavin,

"Doooooo yooooou have a booooooo booooo?"

"No," he replied, "I've fractured my femur."

"Oh my. You have as well." She gave up on small talk after that.

Nurses blew in and out of the room, checking machines, tousling his halo of honey curls, or dropping off stickers. *No news yet.* Finally a nurse gusted in speaking so fast her words melted together like crayons in the sun, "Gavin transfer Children's need clothes pack bag ride ambulance more morphine."

People whirled around us: another shot, a splint, a stretcher, then rolling. I ran to keep up.

The ambulance's windshield wipers batted away small crystals of snow, the kind of flecks that blow into tiny whirls but never stay in one place long enough to drift. Gavin lifted his head to get a better look at the suspension bridge we were driving over.

"I've never been on this bridge before," he declared, straining against the straps that bound him to the stretcher.

"You might be right, Bud," I replied.

"And this bridge has snow," he spoke softly, finger pointed at a swirl of white.

I could only nod my agreement, overwhelmed with the ease in which he found beauty in a bridge and a snowflake.

At Boston Children's Hospital, one person after another entered the room, clipboard in hand—first a nurse, then an intern, then a doctor, maybe even a social worker.

"Tell me *again* what happened."

"What *caused* him to fall from the stool?"

"What were *you* doing at the time of the fall?"

"How exactly *did* he break his leg?"

It might have been the fifteenth time I answered the question, but it felt like the hundredth: "He slid through the back of the breakfast bar stool. The stool landed on him in a heap on the floor."

The same blank stare. The same perfunctory rearranging of equipment. The same wordless exit. Before having Gavin, I worked for a Child Protection Agency. I understood that on paper we looked sketchy: no American medical history, the wrong insurance cards and an unlikely tale of broken bones at breakfast. Despite knowing their protocol, the questions prodded a vulnerable place. I already carried the weight of what I had or hadn't done. I didn't need their interrogation pushing me back to that morning, to our house, to the kitchen. My body was already untethered. Solid to gas. I sublimated.

It's easy to look back, searching for the warning signs, or the moment when you could have stepped in and changed the trajectory of what came next. Disembodied, I listened to the symphony of memory sounds from the morning—my child's chatter (*should I have said quiet down?*), cereal pinging in bowls (*if only I'd made oatmeal*), Simon in the shower (*what if we had all just stayed in bed?*). I searched for the telltale tremble of his cells, their signal of imminent disaster. Instead, all I heard was silence thrumming, like a beating heart, the moment before a sonic boom.

"What happened?" A terse tone snapped me back to the now familiar questions.

I chanted responses that sounded rehearsed.

"Do you realize how unlikely it is that your son would sustain the kind of break he has with your description of events?" The nurse's tone registered somewhere between confused and accusatory.

I exhaled relief and frustration. The alarm was not a result of my unkempt hair or our lack of medical history. It was his body. His twisted bones read nothing like my version of events. This I could understand—the different ways that bodies speak—the way the language of bones can be lost in translation.

In the operating room, Gavin's eyelids fluttered as the anesthetic relaxed his body. I kissed his forehead and, against every mothering instinct, I willed myself to walk away. With Gavin unconscious, there was nothing left binding me together. Cold crept through my shame skin and I unraveled.

Shame sucked the heat from my core. I shivered. No one attempted to soothe the self-pity tempest I conjured. Everyone was battling their own waiting room squalls. Guilt looped in my brain until I dragged myself to the window.

Bits of litter cartwheeled along the sidewalks like elves. Steam swirled from subway grates, wispy ballerinas, en pointe. Winter's pewter sky turned black and tiny balls of gas from millions of miles away ignited like fireflies or campfire sparks. I began to thaw.

Reunited in the recovery room, Gavin seemed more fragile than he had as a newborn. I wanted to scoop him in my arms, but I now required training to hold my son. As he drifted in and out of sleep, I snuck downstairs. The gift shop had none of the things I needed, like underpants, deodorant, and forgiveness. On a whim, I bought a green corduroy dinosaur and joked it was the dinosaur guilt bought. When he woke, Gavin named it Femur.

I'd never been more grateful for the lack of snow than in the weeks that followed Gavin's broken leg. Carrying him in an armpit-to-ankle Spica cast was a challenge without added winter weather obstacles. The snow held off. The day Gavin's cast was removed, flakes pirouetted around his atrophied leg.

"Look!" Gavin spoke with awe. "The snow waited for me."

§

This past September Gavin turned 7. He loves biking and the beach, but he remains steadfastly passionate about, and impatient for, snow. November drizzled and December twinkled. Lights adorned evergreen bushes and snow-free eaves. By the end of January it seemed we were in for another mild winter. Which one of us first joked that, *New England winters aren't really that bad?*

The next day, it snowed. The day after that, it snowed. It snowed and it snowed. It snowed over 108 inches—more than any other winter season in Boston's recorded history.

"Can we go out and play? Please, please, please," Gavin begged.

"Bud, the drifts are taller than you," I pointed out.

It was true, the snow drifted almost to the roof of our house. The quantity of snow did nothing to squelch his thirst for adventures. He pouted.

"Seriously. It isn't safe out there. You could fall and ..." I trailed off.

"I could what, Mum? Break a leg? Ha! Already did that," he chuckled.

He had a point. I grabbed my hat, mittens, and the layers required to tolerate winter. Gavin sensed my acquiescence and slipped into his own wool and weatherproofing.

I watched him scale a sheer wall of snow with an agility and strength I admired, while stifling the churning terror in my chest.

Gavin is strong, I reminded myself. *He is resilient and forgiving. Besides you can't hate the snow forever,* I told myself sternly.

Gavin holds no grudges. It isn't the snow's fault. It doesn't matter what I did or didn't do during that breakfast in the snow. With him, it's just *accidents happen.* I hoard my mother guilt longer.

He packed a snowball together and launched it at me with a quick flick.

"Thanks mum," he said with a smirk.

Snow smeared my glasses and melted on my cheeks. I grabbed his hands and pulled him into a drift. We laughed. Our bodies, chilled to the bone and elated, curled together in the way a child always fits into his mother. Winter cradled us in her snowy arms. Despite the cold, the sun warmed my face and reminded me of the way winter invariably leads to spring.

My Anti-Vegas

Maria Jerinic

My daughter and I are late to spin class. We rush into the crowded parking lot, find the only available parking spot, and leap out. She charges ahead. I stop.

It's snowing.

Large white flakes pour, not sprinkle, down on us, instantly evaporating once they hit the parking lot tar, but still they are there, all around me, white snowflakes.

I drop my keys, and they land at my feet with a clang. My fingers are no longer accustomed to snow-cold. This is Southern Nevada, and I, a former New Englander, have lived here for more than fifteen years.

"Come on" my daughter calls. "We're late." Somehow she is not stunned as I am. Shouldn't this desert-raised child feel wonder at the sight? She doesn't recognize snow even as it falls on her face. To her, it's just cold precipitation, holding her up from the next thing.

She needs me to interpret.

"But it's snowing," I say.

"You're right," she says. She stands under a street lamp and cranes her neck to peer up at the sky. Then she says "but we're late" and charges into the gym.

And I, who rushed us out of the house and delayed dinner because I was determined to make this class, no longer want to go. Snow in Las Vegas is highly unusual. We see snow on the surrounding mountains sometimes. Those that live in the northern part of the city sometimes find a light dusting on their lawns, but where I live, in the south, snow is rare. We still talk about the epic snowstorm of 2008 when schools closed and parts of the city accumulated close to eight inches. On that day, I did not stay home but instead zipped around the city, confident in my driving skills, forgetting that others did not have my experience navigating blizzard conditions. I wanted to see Vegas in the snow.

I love Vegas when it's not Vegas.

Vegas is where the snow birds fly to avoid their hometown winter struggles: the shoveling, the salt, the layers of clothes. Vegas promises ease and play, an escape from the obligations of life. I love that the snow buries these expectations and then forces one to see the other Vegas, the one that is more than a tourist's good time, a mobster's backdrop, a gambler's delight. A Vegas that is more than all of that.

The snow reminds me of the other Vegas, my Vegas, the one, that despite great resistance, I have come to love.

I did not want to move here. I believe the words "over my dead body" were uttered. But there were jobs. In academia, that's hard to overlook, so I moved and said, "it's temporary." Fifteen years later, I am still here.

People tried to cajole me out of my resistance. Natives and long-term residents extolled the virtues of grilling on

Thanksgiving, the constant sun, the pools, 24-hour entertainment. In response, I wondered how I would ever fit in, find my place. The summer heat still leaves me angry and depleted. The casinos, the shows don't interest me. I have come to wear my protests and complaints as a mantle, as an identity. Resisting Vegas is part of who I am. But when the snow comes, I have to ask myself, what can be more lovely than Vegas in this moment?

This is not the Vegas the visitors want. This is not even the Vegas that many residents want. They live here to get away from all that. But for me, in the snow, the Strip lights, which are intrusive and garish, become warm and generous, a welcoming beacon through the mist. In the snow, the lights remind me of the people I have met here, people who are warm and generous, who help keep each other from getting lost.

I love the anti-Vegas.

I love when the sky is grey and the sidewalks are wet and the clouds hang on the mountains that rim the valley. Then, I can smell wet dirt. I love the sight of the city in the early morning on the rare day when the sun hides. There's a pedestrian overpass by my house that my dog and I like to climb. From there we have a Strip view, not the one at night with those fabled lights, but the one I love, the one of buildings rising up on cloudy mornings.

Perhaps Wordsworth prepared me for this ornery love. In college, I found his sonnet "Composed upon

Westminster Bridge, September 3, 1802." Why this poem then? I was ensconced in the Northeast, on an idyllic college campus, complete with ivy-covered gothic buildings shaded by large green trees. Still, the lines moved me:

> Earth has not anything to show more fair:
> Dull would he be of soul who could pass by
> A sight so touching in its majesty.

According to my friend Erik, who knows a lot about these things, this poem is Wordsworth's best. Way back when, in those days when we had time for long beery discussions about poetry, he called this Wordsworth's "antipoem," a term he derived from Yeats's concept of the "anti-self."

For years, I have carried around this description in my mind. Yeats's restless dissatisfaction with his work forced him to challenge his own ways of thinking, or, to cite Erik, to consider how he could "shift his perspective to see what he was missing."

What have I been missing? What have we all been missing?

What had Wordsworth, that Romantic celebrant of daffodils and country people, been missing? In his antipoem, Wordsworth reconsiders his negative view of London, to instead extol its beauties in the early morning: The "[s]hips, towers, domes, theatres, and temples" become as beautiful as the natural world's glories, which only our "dull" "soul[s]" threaten to obscure. But even his own soul needed something to jolt it awake, to see the loveliness—London in the early morning before the usual bustle associated with city streets.

I drive forty minutes to the newish outdoor shopping mall. My daughter loves the uber-trendy natural cosmetic store housed there, and Valentine's Day is coming. I walk in, the only customer on that dark cold February night, and the saleswoman and I hold a gaze, knowing we know but unable to place each other. Then simultaneously, amidst the pink, red, and white bath bombs and soaps, we burst into laughter. She is my student. She'll be in my class in the morning. She frequently rushes in at the last minute. I can tell she's harried, that she balances a lot, but once there, she is always insightful. She is always prepared. She is smart, kind, and thoughtful, and she works very hard.

These connections are everywhere. Vegas is a village made up of people who know you and who know people who know you. Vegas is a village but without the oppressions of a small town. If I want to be anonymous, if I need to slip into temporary obscurity, I can. There is no one watching when I leave a bank or a friend's house. No one will notice where my car is parked. But when I walk into some public space, I may very well meet someone I know.

There is the man at church who recognized my name. He went to graduate school with my father in the Mid-West.

They had not spoken in years.

I finally met the parents of my son's friend, the friend who has my number in his phone and is not afraid to use it. His mother, it turns out, is the mother of a former student. His father's former father-in-law once hired me in another state.

I have so many examples of these ties that I write them down as they appear. I don't want to forget this, the other Vegas, the one made up of overlapping circles.

"See you tomorrow," I tell my student. I hope she gets some rest, and I say that too.

"I will," she says and waves as I leave the store.

Here I celebrate holidays in ways I never did before. The famous Vegas housing market (more square feet for your dollar) provided me with a largely inconvenient house (imagine six bathrooms and four bedrooms but no study) with this saving grace: the living room is so large that I can fit six bookshelves along one wall and many guests can sit at the multiple card tables arranged around the room. At least three times a year, people come from campus, from school, from the playgroup-that-broke-up-ten-years-ago to participate in my inelegant buffets. They eat off paper plates and dodge packs of roving children, now teenagers, and they know they will see each other again at the next event.

My life here resembles Emma's Highbury more than the Rat Pack's playground. I remember my reader's love of literary hosts: Colonel Brandon, thwarted host of the proposed Whitwell expedition; Mr. Knightley, host of the strawberry gathering; Sir John Middleton, host of any-opportunity-for-a party. Who would think I'd find Jane Austen in the Southwest desert?

Certainly there is suffering in Las Vegas. There's a reason for the nickname Lost Wages. Markers of human despair appear everywhere, in the dollar store, on the street corners, on the campus where I teach. Sometimes I think I cannot stay here another day, that my heart will break permanently if I hear about one more runaway, one more overdose.

Our landscaper is a fellow New Englander, a connection we both joyfully acknowledge, and perhaps it's this tie that allows us to discuss politics with civility. One day, the tie stretched thin as we argued over gun control. I felt myself bristling with incredulous irritation at his apparent callousness. "These people," I actually said to myself. And then, somehow, the conversation shifted, and he began to describe a woman he saw arguing with a telephone pole.

"Someone needs to help that lady," he told me, his voice dripping with anguish. "We need to do something. She's out on the street with nothing."

At that moment, I realized there are no "these people." I could not collapse his self, his heart, and his mind into a pre-labeled box. People do not conform to sweeping generalizations.

My perspective shifted.

A former foster child has entered law school not so much for the job security but because someone needs to advocate for those still in care. His generous spirit born of his own suffering inspires me.

My soul is not yet so dull that it can "pass by."

I walk my dog on an early fall evening. It is hot, but not as hot as it was a month ago, and I feel relieved that summer is ending. We are in the middle of the park; there is a soccer game in the near distance, and in between the shouts I hear the incongruous sound of bagpipes. At first I wonder whose iPod is too loud, but then as my dog and I continue, we find him, our piper. He sits in the red dirt, under a fragile, silver stalked shrub, in shorts and a sweatshirt. He sits there and pipes, his haunting tune ushering in the sunset.

My Anti-Vegas.

The First Snow

Alaina Isbouts

It was always a little magical. The little bits of snow appearing out of nowhere, falling softly like the powdered sugar he used to dust over his pancakes in the mornings. Bits of white against a black sky. Gently, calmly, peacefully drifting towards the ground. It built up slowly, and the more it covered the sidewalks, the more it dropped from the sky, heavier, drifting faster, blanketing the ground. The glaze on top of his French crullers on Sundays. The first snow.

I'd always assumed it would be the diabetes that killed him, slowly. It was a selfish disease, always looking for more. First coming for my grandfather's toes, one at a time, until only two remained on each foot. Then it was his leg, just below the knee. But it was the first snow, the first picking up of the shovel that season, that ended his life.

The snow muffled sounds. As if silence fell from the sky. Her cries stifled as he collapsed on the floor of the second story of that corner house. His gasps hushed as he clutched his chest. The ambulance tires quietly crunching through the streets. The muted whispers of neighbors as they saw the stretcher. The quiet voices my father used in the hospital when he called me.

§

25

I knelt in the backseat, turned around so I could peer out the back window. My grandfather was standing there, his face stark, outside that corner house. Dungarees, as he called them, buttoned below his belly, his blood-red Land's End jacket zipped up. He took off his hat, a tweed rain cap from LL Bean he wore daily, and shook the snowflakes from the brim before perching it atop his bald head once again. I waved the excited wave of a child, called out yet another goodbye to him. The car lurched forward as we headed towards the airport. He grew smaller, but before he disappeared, I saw him wipe a tear from his cheek. His lips were pressed firmly together, pulling down at each corner. He was always larger than life. A man who lifted a Volkswagen. A man who once told me bullets bounced off him during the war. But not when we said our goodbyes. When we left, he melted, his layers of frost and ice giving way to a mess of emotions. The snow was grey like the ash from his cigarettes, pushed to the sides of the road.

Now I was the mess of emotions. I pushed through the slush on the sidewalk, too impatient, too consumed by grief, too numb to take the path that was shoveled. The doors of the funeral home were pulled open for me, and before I knew what was happening, I was standing in front of him, cold. I wondered which was colder, the body placed in that casket or how I felt. The windows were frosted shut and over the stale smell of death was the fragrance of lilies, overpowering and out of place in this bitter, empty season

26

of life.

§

It was snowing now, my grandmother's things packed into boxes. I gazed out my kitchen window, watching each flake intently, as I was told the things she would not be moving. Did I want the wooden signs that hung in the dining room? The never-used beer steins that sat for decades over the kitchen cabinets, collecting dust? The antique wash bowl that sat in the corner of her home of sixty years? Who would take the good china? The tears slid down my cheeks and I wondered if they were as unique as the flakes outside. One tear for each year she lived in that corner house. One tear for every child raised there. One tear for each holiday, for each turkey carved, for each rattle of the tambourine on each Christmas Eve, for each present.

She was only moving one block. But it was one block removed from where she lived, in that corner house, in the two bedroom apartment with three children and a husband that planted each rose bush with more love than he showed some of the people in his life. We fought for her to keep her home, but in the end, it was not enough.

§

The snow was everywhere, blanketing everything. My sorrow touched everything, extended to every aspect of my life. It covered me. It was a season of death. Lights twinkled on trees, slowly dying in living rooms. Snow fell. Balloons fell, balls dropped, kisses exchanged on chapped lips. Snow fell. Boxes of chocolates given to lovers, flowers cut at their peak of life to wither and fade in vases, in boxes, delivered to loved ones. Still, snow fell. People died. The trees browned. The flowers wilted.

They had cut roses ready for us, to throw on top of the coffin in the frozen earth. It would be too upsetting, too traumatizing I suppose, to watch them throw on the dirt. And so we threw flowers. I'd picked a rose, as white as the snow collecting on my shoulders, and let it fall gently on top of the lowered box. He'd sent me white roses for my birthday every year. My birthday that year was spent shuffling between that corner house where we had the reception and the funeral home.

We returned from the funeral to the corner house. I had forgotten about the flowers. I closed the door firmly behind me, blocking out the ice and little crystals of broken icicles that blew past me. Boots were kicked off, suitcase thrown down. I no longer had the energy to carry anything. Up the stairs I trudged, my feet feeling heavier with each step I took. On the dining room table, perfectly arranged, a vase of white roses. Before I could even open the card tucked between the stems, I knew they were from him. He'd never miss my Valentine's birthday. He'd ordered them before his heart attack. Flowers from the grave.

No one asked my grandmother to cook. It was her natural instinct, of course, as the mourners gathered in the home she would now live in alone for the first time in her life. She didn't yet know she'd be forced to give up this home, the only home she ever knew with him. *You must be hungry. Let me fix you something.* She shuffled into the kitchen, head lowered, removing containers from the yellowed fridge and bread from the drawer under the coffee pot. Caterers dropped off food, bringing snow and slush into that corner house while people cried quietly in corners. People arrived that I did not recognize with names I'd never heard. Army buddies, the butcher, a senator. Somehow they all seemed to know more about me than I knew about myself.

§

The snow felt heavy and wet. The grief was heavy, and I was unable to carry it all. I felt it all at the first snow. The goodbye we never had. The holidays we'd no longer spend together. The boxes I didn't help pack. That corner house my children would never know. I used to picture my boys running up and down that same narrow hallway in the entry, over that same faded pink rug. Tearing open Christmas presents in the same impatient way that I had thirty years before, on the same pale, faded floral couches wrapped in plastic that had always been there. But he'd never meet my children. He'd always be larger than life, a character in stories I would tell them, growing bigger with each passing Christmas he wasn't there.

That corner house was more than just a house. It was the symbol of our family. Six children of two generations were raised there. Countless grandchildren returned to celebrate, to grieve. Doors were kept unlocked, open to all who needed a place to stay. We'd all taken our turns calling it home. It was a safe haven, a shelter from the frigid harshness of the world. Nothing bad could happen to you in that corner house. But now, we ran from apartment to apartment with snow boots, trying to keep ourselves warm. Trying to keep our family together. It didn't work as well as we'd hoped.

§

He was one of Santa's elves, he said. The big man in the red suit had given him a direct line, all access. He was always the first one to volunteer to stay home with the grandkids while everyone else went to midnight mass. It wasn't that he didn't believe. He abstained from meat on Fridays. Ate only the seven fishes on Christmas Eve. Didn't believe in divorce, especially when my mother filed the papers to leave my father. Wouldn't hear curse words in his home, or watch raunchy movies. But the idea of vulnerability, of someone preaching to him, didn't sit well. He was a man of rules. Not of emotional moments. In his home, feelings were hidden. If a few leaked out of his eye, he'd hastily wipe them off before turning away.

It's Christmas morning and we are all unwrapping

presents. Snow is starting to cover the windows, wrap the balcony, as we sip coffee and crinkle wrapping paper. It is the first Christmas that he is not here. For as long as I can remember, Christmas morning was on the top floor of that corner house. Little—no, nothing—changed until this year. He is not here and my mother is, her first Christmas with my father in fifteen years. My love is here, too; meeting my family, giving us space to process what this snow is reminding us all of, what we are all feeling but cannot say. Our sadness echoed by tears dripping into coffee. My family unwraps my heartache, each gifted photo of him I found in a box after the funeral, blown up and framed. One for everyone, my pain wrapped with shiny red paper, made beautiful with a gold bow.

§

In the haze of the holidays, I forget about the box. It is easily pushed to the back of my mind as I worry about my own house. My own children. The party we host every year and the holiday that is mine to cater now that I have children of my own. The stockings that must be stuffed. The cookies that must be set out, then put back away, leaving only the crumbs out. Enough for the children to see, to notice, to give them enough faith to believe one more year. The anticipation builds, but the holiday is over in an instant, the foreplay of the season drawn out longer each year until we can no longer take it and tear the boxes open. After the wrapping paper has been shoved into the recycling bin, we box up the wreaths and pine-scented candles and twinkle lights, and I notice one last box sitting on the porch. I pick it up, dust snow off the top, and assume it is the last Christmas present, arriving a few days late for the children. I take out a knife and push firmly over the tape, pull out the pages of newspaper cushioning whatever lies inside. But it's not a present. No shiny paper, no glittery bows. It is things from that corner house my mother wanted me to have. A dusty beer stein that was never used. The wooden signs. A porcelain figurine of a little girl, faded and chipped. And once again, as this season does, what glimmer of love I was feeling gives way to heartache.

This is how I see him, still, today. He is forever waving at my father's car as we drive away. Perpetually hiding cigarettes under his cap. Eternally waking me up on Christmas morning, more excited than all of his grandchildren. He is hidden inside each snowflake that falls gently on my front porch as I wrap presents for my own children.

Ice Petal Flowers

Amanda Nevada DeMel

My depression came on gradually at first, then I blinked and found I had no incentive to get out of bed. It was like the snow outside: falling softly when watched, then piling ten inches high by the time the sun rose. Like the blizzard, circumstances piled higher, then a catalyst flung everything into the wild winds. I was climbing out of an ancient, emotional ditch, slothfully, inch by inch, when my best friend, my father, suddenly died. I was twelve years old.

Three months later, lawns and sidewalks were buried in snow, and driveways still had patches of black ice. I came home from an appointment with my therapist, and I thought about the algebra homework due tomorrow.

I let myself out of the car, leaving my mother to brave the icy walk to our front door alone. I could still hear the Grateful Dead playing, since that was always the soundtrack for driving. Shuffling along lifelessly because I lacked the energy and motivation to move at a reasonable pace, I watched the fog of my breath obscure my ratty sneakers and fade seconds later. My father's treasured cacti were sitting outside in a row next to the door. They were gray and brown, withered and dying, unable to survive without their caretaker. I shifted my gaze to where the terracotta pots were, only able to see the tops of the two tallest cacti peeking out of the snow. They looked abandoned, as if forgotten, and I wanted to save them, though I couldn't save myself.

When I discovered that my key was not in my jacket, I sighed and resigned myself to wait for my mother. She was creeping over the ice as slowly as I had, but mostly for safety. She smiled when she saw me staring at her. Her smile was pained. I could only look away in shame. How could I connect with the person I was hurting so badly? For months I had hardly been human; instead I had been a hopeless and depressed mass. There was nothing my mother could do to help me, and she knew that, although she wouldn't give up. I was ashamed of my own futility. That's when I saw it, just barely taller than the snow, just barely rising out of the unforgiving ice.

It was a tiny, purple flower.

I was struck with a line from my father's favorite song: "Glass hand dissolving / To ice petal flowers revolving."

I stared at the flower with more emotion than I had felt in months. My mother finally caught up to me. She unlocked the door and made a joke, asking if I wanted to come in, take off my coat, stay a while. I stared at the little bit of life, unable, or perhaps unwilling, to go inside. My nose was running, and my cheeks were numb. The discomfort didn't push me to move, though. A moment later, my mother saw it. Tears instantly streamed down her face, as if they had been waiting for the right opportunity to emerge.

The flower might have had such an intense effect on her because she believed in signs, messages from the next world. My mother attributed all coincidences and odd occurrences to my father. When she couldn't find something in the house, that meant my father was playing a trick on her. When his favorite song came on the radio, that meant he was saying hello. Of course, she never considered that his favorite song was also one of the most-played songs in the Grateful Dead's repertoire. I knew that she considered the small bloom to be a sign from my father, especially because it was purple, her favorite color. She always smiled whenever she saw a pleasing purple shade, and my father liked to buy her amethyst jewelry. She'd be the first person to say, "That's Daddy looking out for us," so I wasn't surprised when she said it this time. But something was different this time. They were the same words, with the same intention, but I actually considered them for the first time. My vision blurred as my chest constricted.

The next week, I told my therapist about the flower. Although I couldn't say why it moved me so much, I knew it was important to mention. We agreed that believing it was from my father was beneficial and, for the first time, I didn't feel like such a suggestion was ridiculous. In fact, it was a glimmer of inspiration. In that one instance, I felt like a coping mechanism could work.

Seeing the tiny blossom didn't cure my depression, and I still struggle with my father's passing. The flower died before the snow melted, and I've never seen another plant so vibrant in the winter. I don't want to know its species, how it got there, or any other facts about it. If I were to look too deeply into the situation, its mystical nature would disappear. I'd feel alone, isolated, uninspired again. The facts about that flower aren't important. What *is* important is that I saw a flicker of light, accepted a message from my father, and took a step toward healing. Miniscule as the step was, it was progress. It was momentous.

Hidden Light in
Famous Events

Toward Light

Erik Pihel

Thursday, 13 September 2001, 12:30pm
42nd Street F Station, New York

Some of us walked out of the train at 42nd Street. We walked up stairs, through turnstiles, to another staircase. We slowed down, then stopped. A man a few steps above lifted his left crutch onto the next step.

We waited in silence. No one pushed past to get to a meeting.

He lifted his right crutch onto the next step.

No one shouted. No one was in a hurry.

We waited. Maroon tiles colored the staircase walls that led to Bryant Park.

He lifted himself up.

We stepped up.

We were all here together, alive, standing on these steps. There was nowhere more important to rush off to. There was nothing more important than to wait for this man to climb to 42nd Street. The world was fragile. We were fragile. We were assholes. But not today.

He lifted the left crutch onto the next step.

No one spoke. People above waiting to descend stood still. No one pushed through to catch the next train. A man just above the climber waited, pressing himself into the maroon tiles to make more room.

We would wait here with him for eternity.

He lifted the right crutch onto the next step.

We had always stood on these steps, patiently waiting, but didn't know until something drastic woke us up.

He lifted himself up.

We were awake. We were grateful for the privilege of waiting for this man. We were grateful for sidewalks and streetlights, for volunteers giving coffee cups to diggers, for the sun streaking maroon tiles with stripes of gold.

He lifted the left crutch onto the next step.

There was no rush.

He lifted the right crutch onto the next step.

New York was silent and still.

Our leader lifted himself up.

We quietly stepped up, slowly, slowly climbing toward light.

Long Distance Loss

Emily Skelding

Who do you cry with when no one in your day-to-day knows the person you lost? What do you say in a card to a family you never met? How can you grieve a friend who dies in a war zone, in a conflict you barely understand?

Memories of Jim, often of little significance, hit me at unexpected times. When I see a man with so much product in his hair that a comb leaves lines, hours after he's styled it, I think of Jim.

Once in a Starbucks, I stood behind a man about his size wearing a shirt fresh from the dry cleaner's hanger. I could tell the man was smiling at everyone who passed because as the people moved by they could not help but grin at him or at least nod and give a half-smile back. I thought for a moment: is Jim here? He must be on a trip to New Orleans for a journalism conference, waiting in front of me to order his coffee before he heads off to give the keynote. Then I remembered: that would be impossible.

Whenever I see a pool noodle, one of the few that litter our backyard where the above-ground pool used to be or fifty standing tidily yet droopily on the deck at my children's swim lessons, I think of Jim. The first time I encountered a noodle was with him. Jim convinced me to sneak into a resort pool late one night. Half a dozen of us or so, no longer in college and not yet sure how to be anything but carefree students, half-wrestled and half-sword fought with the new pool toys as our weapons. The pool lights were bright, but we were wise enough to not be so loud we'd be discovered. I remember thinking the new-fangled fad would stand the test of time. I hoped my friendship with Jim would too.

Most days I wear a silver cuff on my wrist. I have about half a dozen. The one my daughter gave me with the word "love" etched into it, the one from my trip to Cuba, and the one with a *fleur-de-lis* stamp nestled together with others in a cigar box in the top drawer of my dresser. When I open the box to put on the bracelet I wear most days, a spoon bent and beaten to fit my wrist, I see my first one. It is small and thin and smooth. Jim was with me when I got it. We were washing our clothes at a laundromat and wandered into a second-hand store next door. It cost $10, which seemed pretty steep, but Jim told me to get it, so I did. I wear it so rarely that when I do, people ask if it is new. I tell them I've had it for over twenty years but don't mention Jim.

In August of 2014, Jim was murdered in front of the world on YouTube. His death was the top news story for weeks. One of the early headlines read "James Wright Foley, Kidnapped Journalist, Apparently Executed by ISIS." Pictures of Jim were everywhere. People talked about his death as they knew it, a tragic and incomprehensible story the media bombarded us with. Most people in my day-today did not know I knew Jim.

I was left to grieve on my own.

§

On most Sunday afternoons, I feel a wave of angst. After the quiet reflection of church and before the breakneck pace of the week is thrust on me, I worry. My weekend is never as restful as I expect it to be, the tasks of the week fill my head and interrupt my train of thought, and there is nothing in the fridge to be packed as weekday lunches for my four children.

On one of these Sundays, just over a year after Jim was killed, I faced a task. Jim's family created a foundation in his name to advocate for kidnapped hostages, protect conflict journalists, and educate the world about the hostage crisis and the danger freelance, conflict journalists face. I follow the foundation's work on social media. Every year the foundation hosts a 5K race in Jim's home state of New Hampshire and a virtual race around the world to bring attention to their cause and raise money. People around the world run the race in solidarity. I planned to run a race all by myself at home in New Orleans.

On the day I planned to complete the 5K, I tried to nap and failed, so I put on a t-shirt with Jim's silhouette and the hashtag #irunforJim. I don't usually run. Occasionally I jog, but it is really a trot. I prefer yoga and biking, but that day I ran a 5K I mapped for myself along the streetcar line. I dreaded going outside and breaking a sweat, preferring to wallow in my anxieties.

But as a jaded forty-one-year old, I knew not to trust my impulse to do nothing. The usual dread of the week is never resolved by dwelling on it. I needed a break. The streetcar that runs from the edge of the French Quarter and under the oak trees of Uptown ends a few blocks from my house. Running on the soft ground between the rails is easier on my knees than the asphalt loop at the park. I thumped along the dirt path, outpaced by the regular runners, comforted to be channeling my Sunday unease into a pointed and doable task.

The turn-of-the-week unrest has plagued me for all of my adult life. In the first years of playing at being grownups, when Jim and I were first year teachers with Teach for America in Phoenix, we lesson-planned through those worries. We sat in outdoor-mall coffee shops under misters, trying to ignore the shoppers and stay focused on crafting a performance for the thirty eager middle schoolers who awaited us the following morning.

We were out of our depth, idealists, part of Teach for America's second group of teachers to work in the city. There were about thirty of us in a city of over a million, yet we hoped to make equity in education a reality in two short years.

We didn't know what we didn't know. Everyday in the classroom was like going to battle with pool noodles, when we needed an appropriate curriculum and experience with our school communities and wisdom beyond our years. Maybe our students liked us. They hung out in our classrooms when we weren't teaching, but while we were teaching, chaos often ensued. Crayons or pencils were broken and thrown across the room; the most capable children interrupted and told us bluntly how to better run their classroom, and the quietest students grew quieter and more withdrawn. Teach for America's motto, to make sure all children have access to excellent education, was our mantra, and we were falling short.

I took myself too seriously. I arrived at school by 6:00am, partly because I couldn't sleep and partly because I was inefficient, spending two hours perfecting what turned out to be a fifteen-minute lesson and leaving hours of class time not structured enough. I was fixated on my ineptitude. Most of the Teach for America teachers taught elementary school. Jim and I were placed in middle school.

Jim knew how to break up the weight of the failure we faced. While he shared with me the despair he felt, he laughed at our preposterous situation and poked fun at our earnestness. While I wanted to fall asleep on Friday night after Happy Hour and work all weekend, he made plans, danced at clubs, and invited people over to his house. He joined a gym and made non-teaching friends while he was working out. On Sunday, we'd often meet up, try not to fret, and get organized for the week.

Jim and I first met just weeks after college graduation, during our five weeks of teacher boot camp in Houston. My first impression of Jim--he was too friendly, smiling at everything. He attempted small talk.

I rolled my eyes, "We probably won't even end up being friends, so why are you asking me where I went to college?"

That night we shared a pack of Marlboro Lights I bought from a machine by the bathrooms. Jim had no pretense, nothing to prove. His grin was not pomp. He liked almost everybody. We rode home together in the way back of someone's hatchback.

At the time of Jim's death, I had a baby, a toddler, and two teenagers. I could not fly to the funeral or hunker down in bed for a week. While reading the latest reports on Jim as often as I could refresh my phone, I nursed the baby on the couch, in my minivan at school dismissal, and twice in the middle of the night. Dinners were made, and teenage moods endured while my heart ached and mind spun.

Friends I saw regularly for playdates didn't know I lost an old friend. I didn't bring it up. Instead of talking, I scribbled down every moment of Jim. Each memory revived another. I was afraid moments I recalled with sudden clarity might fade.

Phoenix is a sprawling city punctuated by a mountain range rising out of stucco subdivisions. These rocky desert peaks tower over miles and miles of a tidy grid of manicured malls and Mexican restaurants. Jim and I taught in South

Phoenix, where the houses were smaller, the streets had pedestrians, and the yards were full of children. My life alternated between the constant panic of knowing I was failing my students and longing for my boyfriend who was studying in England. There was never enough time to grade papers, and I ended my days with solo visits to my apartment complex's treadmill. I was playing at being a professional in linen dresses, which I wrinkled on the way to work with a messenger bag slung across my chest. I thought it looked like a briefcase. I missed my backpack.

I have a picture of Jim and me dancing from this time. Jim is in the foreground, loose-limbed, grooving. You can't see his face, but it is unmistakably him, lost in the music. I am in the background, kicking my leg out at a right angle. My hair is mid-toss. We are worn from a week in the trenches, reviving ourselves in someone's bare bones apartment.

I showed my teenagers the picture. My daughter asked about the denim mini-skirt I was wearing, and my son marveled that the guy in the photo was the one in the news.

Once when Jim and I were in a convenience store buying our Marlboro Lights, I mentioned I'd never had malt liquor. Jim bought me my first and only Olde English 40. We drank them sitting on a sidewalk, wondering if our teaching would ever be "better than subs." We took late night swims. We slogged through weeknight ESL certification classes sitting in the back row, passing notes. We went to the movies.

One of Jim's brothers, the one who looks just like him, visited Phoenix. The three of us hiked up South Mountain. Along the rocky path, between the cacti, we came across several javelinas, strange pig-like animals with tusks who run in wild herds. Jim tried to chase them and scare them off. His brother and I stood frozen. Later we learned they can be extremely dangerous when threatened. This seemed to sum up those years in Phoenix: not knowing what we were up against and pushing ahead anyway.

Jim talked about his family: four brothers and a little sister, all his younger siblings, a Catholic family done right. I wanted a family like his, a family requiring weeknight dinners at a long table.

My 40th birthday was six days after Jim's death. I canceled a night out with my husband and my in-laws, favoring cake at home with our children. It hardly seemed right to celebrate when there was an empty seat at the Foley's table. Mainly, I was tired. Shouldn't I be in a dark church on my knees? Or reading a serious book about the shifting situation in Syria? Or watching a weighty movie to make myself cry?

The summer in between my two years in Phoenix, Jim and I went on separate trips to Mexico. One night I went to a discotech, trying to feel at home with people I'd just met. The dance floor was circled by four balconies. Jim ended up in the same city in the same club with his new friends. He spotted me from above and wove his way through the crowd. He tapped me on the shoulder and asked if I had a cigarette. I screamed, but no one but Jim could hear me above the music. I abandoned the guy I was dancing with and gave Jim a big hug.

The following year was my final year in Phoenix. Jim was staying, and I was moving to the Bay Area to be with my boyfriend.

In July, the month before my move, Jim and I teamed up to train fresh new teachers. The third week of the training, I realized my period was late. The only person I told was Jim. About a week later, one Sunday morning, I woke up to an entirely new feeling in my body: a stretching, a tightening, and a tenderizing in my lower belly and breasts. I tried to reach my boyfriend and left a voicemail on his sister's answering machine. I took a test. When it was positive, I went numb. Jim stopped by my dorm room.

He knew the moment he laid eyes on me but asked me nothing directly.

"Are you ok?" I told him no.

"Have you talked to Phil?" I told him no.

Jim walked me downstairs and bought me pizza and a grape Hi-C. He sat with me and watched me eat, gracefully keeping others at bay. He helped me craft just the right lie to get out of our nightly meeting. He told me not to worry and didn't hint at his own anxiety.

When he walked me back to my room, there was a voicemail from my boyfriend, Phil. Jim left, and I made the call. By the next morning Phil had traveled across several states, finding his way to me. By mid-September we were married, and in March of the following year, our son was born.

The next summer, Jim came and visited us in Oakland and met our son. He was checking up, making sure marriage and family were working out okay for me.

In the weeks and months after Jim's death, I obsessively read public remembrances of him. Like me, people connected to Jim in tough times, because Jim put himself in tough situations. One day, I heard a voice I knew on NPR. It was one of Jim's roommates, Daniel, another Phoenix corps member. Daniel, a poet, described his grief. He wanted to break Jim's nose when he came home "the first time" after being held in Libya. "The first time" stuck with me. We all knew Jim would return a second time. Jim told Daniel he'd played it safe when he left for Syria. I wished he'd stuck to his promise.

After several weeks of grieving on my own, I knew I needed to share my loss. I reconnected with some friends from Phoenix on Facebook and tracked down another using her mother's home number found in a long unused address book. A friend I knew in New Orleans had another acquaintance who knew Jim. This stranger called, and we talked for an hour about our friendships with Jim in different decades in opposite corners of the country. We were all in shock.

Talking reminded me I was the only person to show up to Jim's "Dress Like Your Student" party and the times we met up to hear the blues at the Rhythm Room on Indian School Road. Each story breathed life into other memories I'd forgotten.

I continued to write notes about Jim for months, poring over them. Eventually I cleaned them up and sent them to Jim's family with a note of condolence. His mom emailed back within the hour, urging me, "Treasure your children … hold them tight."

The last time I shared a beer with Jim was over eleven years ago. We bumped into each other at a Teach for America conference in DC. When we saw each other we lit up and hugged tight, chuckling at nothing—just like when we'd found each other in the discotech. He was writing fiction and teaching in prison, adjusting to Chicago and missing Phoenix.

I was at the conference networking because our family was moving from Boston to New Orleans. It was just months after Katrina. My parents, our grad school advisors, friends, and the guy who sat next to me on the airplane, advised against the move.

While we were supposed to be listening to the keynote speakers, Jim leaned over to me, "You should move to New Orleans. You should definitely do it. You'll never regret it."

I showed him pictures of our two children, seven and four at the time. He lingered on the snapshots and turned to a friend on the other side of him, "That's really something, isn't it?"

I wish I could have made it to Jim's memorial with our fourth baby strapped to my back. Funerals help me process loss because when I share in the story of a life, I like to linger on the last chapter. At a life's end, as I place the narrow volume of a friend's time here on the shelf, I long to be back on the first pages, wondering how things might develop, diverge, and conclude. I want to talk his life over with the rest of the people who knew Jim.

I want to bump into him again, at a club in New Orleans or on a visit to Boston.

On the Sunday of the virtual race, fourteen months after he was killed, in my #irunforjim gear, I run past tourists perched on the tracks that turn at the Riverbend. Some of them don't realize the Mississippi River is flowing by, a few hundred feet away, hidden by the levee. The levee is deceptive. It seems like a grassy knoll, a spot designed for folks to run their dogs. In fact, this bend in the river is one of the spots where the Mississippi refuses to accommodate a neat grid for New Orleans streets. New Orleans' thoroughfares Carrollton and St. Charles end at the river. Its nature will not accommodate a tidy layout. We must bend to it.

Losing Jim has been like this. I am moving through life, passing folks who are unaware of a hidden friendship, which ended too soon, forcing me to bend.

I'm not good at staying in touch with people who live far away. I've moved too much, had too many kids, and don't have time for long phone calls. It'd be weird to suddenly text or video chat with someone I knew before those technologies were at our fingertips. I wait to see people in person. When I travel to a place near a kindred spirit, I look them up. It amazes me how across the years and despite the ways our lives digress from one another, if we finally quit the end-of-day cigarette or if we become all-day smokers, we recapture the spirit which was always there between us. I assumed Jim and I would have a chance to catch up again. I'd show him the latest photos of my children, and he'd encourage me to keep writing, to pick what feels like the dangerous and true path.

My face turned red when I ran. Getting my heart rate up energized me. This surprised me. I did not train for the race, but I was able to drag myself along. The rattle of the streetcar didn't distract me from my recollections of Jim. I hopped from one moment to another, grateful to have shared so many smokes with him. I was part of a team of runners, all part of the original group of Teach for America teachers in Phoenix. Some people on our virtual crew were in Boston, another was in Argentina, and another felt almost close in Atlanta.

Jim's virtual run has become a yearly tradition for me. I am building a collection of t-shirts with Jim's image. Every fall people all over the world run for Jim.

And still, I am alone, missing him.

The Heart of the City
Ligia de Wit

Thursday, September 19th, 1985

I am no rookie to earthquakes.

My first one was exciting. Or so my sixteen-year-old self thought. September 19th, 1985, 7:15am. I was about to take a class on campus when the second floor of the building swayed from side to side.

Cool, my first earthquake!

Two hours later, we found out that it was an 8.1 earthquake that hit south of where I was. Entire buildings flattened like pancakes. Ten thousand dead, though the numbers varied, and some said twenty thousand. A baseball stadium was used to dump all the bodies.

Mexico City was built on a lakebed. Who the heck decided to build a city on a lake? But that's another story. I lived in the suburbs—outside the lakebed, where the ground is solid—and I felt it like a gentle rocking.

Hearts in our throats, tears in our souls, the next day we went from house to house to collect donations, anything. I didn't think it was fun. "Cool" was far from my mind.

We were scared. Bruised.

Tuesday, September 19th, 2017

Today at 11am, a general drill has been scheduled to

commemorate the '85 earthquake. My back hurts, and with my office situated on the 5th floor, I ponder taking the elevator instead of the nasty emergency stairs. My sore back wins and I cheat, leaving five minutes early. I meet with two coworkers, hanging out by the building's Starbucks.

"Some brought flats and changed their shoes," one complains. "Cheaters. An earthquake doesn't announce in time for us to bring flats."

Or take the elevator five minutes earlier.

The high-pitched seismic alarm blares and we follow the instructions to walk out of the eight-story building, hang out until everyone's accounted for, then we all return to work. Just another drill, a special one that everyone did in Mexico City at the same hour.

The seismic alarm goes on again. And again.

"Oooh, didn't we do the drill right?" I joke. "Do we need to repeat this?"

The operations manager grins. "Nah, it's malfunctioning."

An hour and a half later, I feel the building move and hold my breath.

Everyone stands up, tense. The fear builds to a palpable weight as the shaking increases. A strong earthquake on the same day that we commemorate the devastating '85 one?

The operations manager shouts, "Everyone to the columns. Now!"

Because of the '85 earthquake, our building's

suspension is hydraulic. On the fifth floor, you feel it in your bones since the suspension absorbs the impact and it's like a slinky toy. It's 1:15pm and the building sways from side to side.

The frames on the walls move like piñatas. The woman at my side hyperventilates and one of my coworkers soothes her.

It's the strongest earthquake I've ever felt. *If here, where the ground is solid, the earthquake is being felt so strongly, so crazily powerful … what is happening in Mexico City?*

My mind goes back to '85 and my throat closes. My kids should be safe—they are on solid ground like my building, but what of the millions of people trapped in the buildings on the lakebed, including my sister, who lives there?

My husband! He's always driving all over the city. Is he okay?

I push the thought away. No time for hysterics.

The shaking finally stops. We walk down the stairwell. I lift my skirt carefully to avoid tripping, noticing a bit of rubble, cracks, hairline fractures in the walls I've never seen before.

Another coworker sobs behind me. We must stay calm. Buildings never fall in this area but … *what if this one does?*

We are directed to the empty McDonald's lot next to us. We didn't do that in the drill.

"Don't use cellphones, people," a woman with a bright vest shouts, stopping the heavy traffic so we can go to safety.

"Keep walking until you reach safe ground!"

Everyone is on their cells. But the lines are dead. There's no one on the other side. Lines collapse as they do every time an earthquake hits.

WhatsApp works. Thank God!

Is everyone alright? I text my family.

My sister is safe. Everyone answers. Except my husband.

Where are you? I text him.

I glance around, trying to bide time and hope that he's fine. He must be.

A couple of minutes and he texts back. *I'm just beside your building. Pick you up just ahead.*

It turns out he was driving by when the alarm sounded on his radio and people from my building poured onto the freeway. God does work in mysterious ways.

My daughter is on the same campus where I felt the earthquake thirty-two years ago, and thought it was fun. She doesn't think it is. She's all right and so are her fellow students.

My husband and I pick up my son, who strides out of his school, his tall and lean figure quickly approaching. Despite his teenage-y efforts of hiding his anxiety, his relief is evident when he sees me.

"Mom, Dad! Where's my sister? Grandma?" His face contorts into that seriousness he's known for, a steely determination behind his eyes. I notice how he's turning into a man. "*Where* is Grandma?"

My mom had been in one of the most affected areas just a few days ago. She's now at her home, safely away.

Social media broadcasts news about the earthquake. A video goes viral and we see a building collapse in a cloud of dust. Many more threaten to do the same.

We want to help, yet the city has frozen. "Stay at home, those who can," they broadcast everywhere. "If you want to help, stay put. Keep the roads clear for the ambulances and military."

All my family is well. Too many families aren't.

Being in the suburbs, I'm far away from the affected area. I feel helpless. Buildings are threatening to collapse. "Please, stay at home," volunteers keep repeating on social media. "We have enough help here." Facebook, text messages, and whatever communications we can use, help to reach out, and we're attentive to what is said by those in the thick of disaster.

I can hardly believe this is happening. We've been hit by a lot of earthquakes since that terrifying '85 one with no damage until now.

Hundreds of young people pour into the streets. They tweet and post what's needed and where. My hope blossoms at a breathtaking picture that I see on Facebook: thousands of donated water bottles cover the ground, plastic blue spreading in all directions like a glittering clear sea under the sunlight. "Please don't send more water. We need these types of medicines ..."

The pictures and videos lift our spirit. Hundreds of volunteers help get people out. It takes hours and the military arrives, working alongside the civilians, who refuse to leave until everyone is accounted for.

I wonder how many lives would have been saved if that drill had been at 1pm. But that didn't happen and it's no use to ask myself this. Even as I do.

§

Next day, without access to my work building, I go to Home Depot to buy gloves, helmets, or shovels. There are none. I go to the drugstore for medicines they've requested. Empty shelves. Lots of good souls are sending them to hundreds of impromptu gathering points that young people have organized. They're everywhere with huge cardboard messages: "Mexico, we need your help."

"Millennials have seized the city," older people post. "We hope they don't let go."

A squat two-story building near my house is turned into a gathering point. Three young volunteers started it. The following day, dozens help. Trucks arrive. Human chains are organized, and the nearby Starbucks is full.

The heart of the people beats strong. Unyielding.

"Please, go home, we have enough help," the rescuers say to volunteers wanting to remove collapsed building rubble and rescue the people trapped inside.

"We'll wait. Those helping now will tire. We'll be here."

Where the trucks can't go, motorbikes show up, zooming paramedics through the city where huge blocks are restricted to traffic. Some detour cars and try to organize the chaos.

The heart of the city beats.

Citizens open their houses to shelter those who lost theirs. Restaurants give free food. Young volunteers on the street collect help. Human chains of neighbors don dust-masks, working to take out huge blocks of cement to rescue those under them. They risk their own lives to save whoever is in need—selfless souls helping, proving wrong the notion that we don't care about our neighbor. My throat closes and tears brim my eyes.

Rescuers lift a fist, asking for silence. They hear someone. Everyone in the area keeps silent, even those of us watching the TV from the safety of our houses. Our eyes stick to the screen, holding our breath and not daring to move. A prayer harbors in my chest while my joined fingers press my lips. The silence is heavy, yet a light pulses within. Hope.

I see a woman—first her feet, then her body—pulled down from a hole in a roof, like giving birth. My breath releases. Her face shows the agony she lived in the past hours and her wild hair is full of dust. But she's alive.

We hear unsettling news from my daughter's sister campus. "The bridges connecting buildings were destroyed." My daughter shows me a video where bridges fall down during the earthquake. Who had the heart, the nerve, to record this at that moment? The new generation hardly puts its smartphones away and that recording was probably second nature.

An image of a tall, dark-haired, handsome nineteen-year-old pops up on Facebook. He smiles at the camera at the Louvre in Paris. He looks vivacious and ready to take on the world. "Have you seen him?" He's a student of the collapsed campus. My heart cries out and we know at least one student is dead. I hope it's not him.

§

Devastating news hits us. An elementary school in the city collapsed completely. Some children made it out alive. The heart of the city holds its breath and we all keep our attention glued to the television since there is news of one little girl texting from within, waiting for her rescue. Frida Sofia. Mexicans tremble and cry along with the reporter, who's been more than thirty hours at the site without sleeping, as well as dozens of people outside. We whisper her name, praying for her to come out safe. They say she texts that two other children are nearby, alive.

The rain pours. My heart aches even more. We have no relief from Mother Nature. Our famous volcano, the Popocatepetl, erupts ashes. He's a warrior legend from yore who decides to stay put for the moment. He might not want to wake up Iztaccihuatl, our Sleeping Woman—a beautiful

Aztec legend of our twin volcanoes overlooking Mexico City.

Citizens don't leave their posts. Trembling tarps are lifted to protect the rescuers from the unforgiving sheets of rain. *Damn, I should have bought raincoats.* We had them in our hands, but I thought it ridiculous then that it'd rain.

Then suddenly, after agonizing hours and all Mexico holding its breath, praying for the souls of those little ones, the news about the school vanishes. No one reports anything.

"What happened?"

The military running the operation say that every child is accounted for: alive with their parents in the hospitals or heartbreakingly dead.

There is no Frida Sofia. There never was.

Some say it was a collective hysteria and someone picked up the wrong information. Some, more cynical, said that the TV channel tried to make a soap opera out of it. People are enraged. We feel betrayed. I'm sure the reporter, after more than thirty hours standing outside, is emotionally devastated. I know I am—that news breaks our heart and hope.

Thirty-two children died and I can't even think of this without feeling a dark hole within me. The pain of the parents can't be soothed away.

That doesn't stop the people.

Canta, México, no llores. "Sing, Mexico, don't cry."

Impromptu writers flood the media. "Let me hug you, Mexico." Their beautiful inspiring words lift our spirits. Draw tears out of our red eyes. And we smile. We smile because we realize that our people are stronger, braver, more tireless than any of us have thought.

They say you know who a person is in the face of disaster. And we see what we are made of.

We find out that five students died on my daughter's sister campus. One of them pushed his girlfriend to safety as the rubble came down. She lives. I can't imagine the burden on her young shoulders as she knows he's not coming out of that rubble.

The dark-haired handsome boy is dead too.

Four-legged heroes appear in the media. Frida, Evil, and Ecko help, wearing goggles and curious socks. Frida alone finds more than fifty people in the rubble. They're alive thanks to this beautiful, courageous dog, which oddly is named like the non-existent Frida girl.

We all love her. Her picture invades social media, representing hope. Foreign countries send rescue parties, even a British firefighter who came to help of his own accord: a man with a big mustache and proud eyes—our honorary Mexican. We praise him. Praise all. We thank you all and we are indebted.

§

Earth's rage isn't over yet. We Mexicans know by experience

that, after a strong earthquake, another comes on its heels. We hold our breath. One-hundred aftershocks and counting. Nothing serious.

Saturday at 8am, it comes. A 6.1. Nothing major but a bridge that was already damaged collapses. Perhaps other damaged buildings suffer further damage. Death toll: two women who die of heart attacks.

"I want to give these candies to those helping out," a little girl says to her parents. She gives her candies to the hard-working, relentless people. You're never too young to help.

"I want to help too," says an old woman who gives free massages to those heroes right on the street. You're never too old, either.

I'm at home, safe on solid ground and away from the devastation. Yes, I've donated. Yes, I bought medicines and helpful stuff. And yet, I wish I was there in the city helping. I feel frustrated. So I write.

The death toll so far is about four hundred. A tragedy, yes, although a far cry from the thousands back in '85.

More than forty buildings collapsed in the first twenty-four hours. Some collapsed later and too many are damaged. Many people have lost their homes entirely—there's no home insurance habit in us.

There is change though. We're not the same since that '85 disaster. We've grown. I hope that these winds of change keep blowing and lifting our spirits.

Tuesday, September 26th, 2017

A week after the earthquake, there's a ceremony at my daughter's campus to remember their five fellow students. Why do five young men affect me more than the hundreds? They were young and had their lives in front of them. They're just about the age of my kids and that hits home. I could be living my life without them and I can't bear that weight. My pain goes to those who must do so.

And I saw his face on Facebook and prayed for him to be alive. Because his careless smile still haunts me. Haunts his parents too.

They ask for a minute of silence. A sea of fists is raised in honor of those young men. White balloons are released into the sad sky. Then they list each of the five students' names and, throat tight, students say, "We are one" after each one is named. God rest their souls.

The earthquake hit. And it hit us hard. But the phoenix that rose from the rubble is magnificent. The true spirit of the Mexicans came alive. It shone, bright and hopeful. Beautiful.

The earthquake not only collapsed buildings and destroyed the homes of so many. It also unveiled the true heart of the city. A heart that pulses, vibrates. That feels. A heart that has been hidden for too long.

The aftermath is still here. Our warrior volcano is still fuming and people are nervous. Buildings are still damaged. The news of a possible new earthquake unnerves us. But the spirit and heart of the city beats strong in the young, in everyone lending a hand. So many stories to be inspired by, including that of a soldier weeping bitterly as he retrieves a dead girl and the father searching for him until he finds the soldier. "Thank you for returning my daughter to me."

Let me never forget who the Mexicans really are.

Today, I lift a fist to Mexico. I lift a fist to its spirit, to its warriors who didn't fail or hesitate when they were most needed.

I lift a fist to those who didn't eat, rest, or blink until they did all they could to rescue those beneath tons of cement.

I lift a fist to its heart.

As the World We Knew Burned

Fran Braga Meininger

I watched as the wind whipped the oaks above me, sleepless with worry, expecting to hear the crack of a branch crashing through my roof at any moment. But it was something far more ferocious and insidious that sprang me from my bed at 1:00am. First, I heard sirens, then noticed an eerie glow beyond the trees to the north. Fire.

I dressed in a rush, peered out every window, but couldn't get a clear view. I grabbed my keys, called my dog to follow me and ran for the car. As I drove around the curve to the highway, the vista opened up to reveal the flames, already engulfing the entire ridge of the Mayacama Mountains and burning down toward the valley floor. I feared for the safety of friends who lived within the bounds of the fire, but I was helpless to do more than send hope for their safety. I had no time to spare. The wind was driving the flames my way. I drove back through shards of eucalyptus bark swirling through the air and dodged branches that littered the roadway. My heart pounded as I made a mental list of what I needed to pack.

I announced the situation to my husband, who refused to share my concern. I tried in vain to convince him of the impending danger as the fire moved ever closer and my phone lit up with messages from neighbors preparing to evacuate. I could see in his expression that he was sure I was overreacting. Finally, knowing time was running out, I split the emergency cash with him and delivered an ultimatum; he could leave with me now, or I was going without him. I went without him.

Lesson #1: ultimately, I am only responsible for myself.

With the dog settled in the back seat, a small bag hastily stuffed with clothes, phone, charger, water, a flashlight and a box with yearbooks and photos, I drove away not knowing if I would ever return to my home of twenty-three years.

Lesson #2: when it's imperative, I know what's important.

I drove into town with no destination, only a primal instinct to get away from the flames. I was not alone; many others headed into Sonoma in the dark of night, the glow growing distant in the rear-view mirror. But as I drove south, I found the eastern horizon also lit up, from fires burning on the same mountain range.

I pulled into the high school parking lot to get a clear view and found a group huddled together, exchanging information and kind words. I joined them. We were each from a different part of the valley and different financial circumstances reflected in the row of vehicles parked side by side—a beat-up pick up, a ranch truck with vineyard tools in the back, a Tesla and my Prius, but in that moment, it didn't matter. We were fellow humans sharing a devastating situation and offering each other comfort.

Lesson #3: in the face of adversity kindness and

compassion prevail.

Finally, a call from my husband, who had seen for himself that the situation was indeed as dire as I'd reported. The fire was now burning only a few hundred yards from our house. He was on his way.

I drove through town in search of companionship and a coffee. The Safeway parking lot was full of people milling about looking up at the horizon, making calls as they watched the glow increase in area and intensity. A few ladies sat inside at the closed Starbuck's counter. Not having anywhere else to go and not wanting to be out there alone, I joined them. I monitored the situation on social media, listening as they recounted their experiences and voiced concerns for those who would not leave and those from whom they had not heard. It was universal. Everyone was more concerned for others than themselves.

The magnitude of the situation still had not quite sunk in. I honestly expected to return to my normal life after a few hours of fear and uncertainty.

My husband finally arrived. We stocked up on fresh fruit, water and snacks to sustain us for a few hours and exchanged messages with neighbors who were now out of the fire zone and checking in. With Starbucks still closed, we decided to see if we could find coffee and with it the comfort of normalcy.

A sidewalk café on the Plaza was open and crowded. We sat, our faces buried in our phones, searching for updates and shared what we found with those at other tables. When everyone related from where they had just evacuated, it became acutely apparent how widespread the fires were. They extended far beyond the boundaries of our valley. Fourteen fires burned simultaneously: to the east In Napa, to the west in Bennett Valley and to the north in Santa Rosa. The world we knew was burning.

A friend sent a message offering breakfast and the chance to watch the news coverage. I spent the next few hours watching the visual evidence of the widespread destruction, but what troubled me the most was the personal loss and intimate pain of those I knew and loved. The fire erupted with such fury that people fled their homes with only their loved ones and pets and the rest was now scattered as ash.

Lesson #4: the reaction to tragedy comes in waves.

I watched in horror, a drama that couldn't possibly be real, as my heart broke. A reflex response shook it off. There was no time to grieve. I had to plan and react. But I noticed an unfamiliar lack of focus and the inability to make a definite decision. I was devoid of the energy to rally and push through whatever I had to face. I felt the first sense of defeat.

Lesson #5: there are times when powerlessness is inevitable and unavoidable.

The next few days melted together. The sky, normally vibrant blue and alive with the soft autumn breeze, was now oddly still and heavy with an unearthly orange haze that blocked the sun and cast long, surreal shadows, obscuring what was familiar and comforting. Gigantic plumes appeared, seemingly everywhere, around us. A new one declared the flames had flared up in another location. We were losing the battle.

We sought new shelter as the fire expanded, staying with friends, only to be evacuated, along with them, as their homes were threatened. My most important tools were my phone and my laptop, which the writer in me threw in the bag as I rushed out the door knowing I'd need to write.

Practically everyone I loved was within the fire zone. My close circle was displaced just as I was. There was not a safe haven among us. We had been scattered in the wind like the ash of the fire that chased us from our homes, our serenity and our security. But we stayed connected with constant calls, Facebook posts, texts and emails.

Lesson #6: no matter where you go, those you love travel with you.

As the fire grew to the largest in recent history, consuming hundreds of thousands of acres and destroying most of what it touched, I found myself oddly passive. There was no anger, no rage. My usual spirited reaction to anything that frightened or threatened me was gone. I couldn't fight this. It was bigger, stronger and more threatening than any defense I could muster. I had to admit defeat, run and simply adapt to whatever it left in its wake.

I felt an unfamiliar resolve to the possibility that my house was gone. I had no idea what I might do if that were true. I simply did not have the energy or imagination to conjure up the multiple scenarios necessary. I could only settle into the security of a temporary sanctuary and the knowledge that everyone I loved was safe, for now.

Lesson #7: life isn't meant to be pushed around and sometimes when it gets tough, you just can't fight back.

On the fifth night of its constant consumption in all directions, through every hill surrounding us, the fire threatened the entire town of Sonoma. My childhood girlfriend in tow, my husband and I moved farther west. I once again drove away from the flames, without a plan, knowing there was no other choice than to gather up the few things that represented my tentative security and flee once again. Welcomed by relatives, we settled in and watched the reports through the night, hoping the center of our tightly knit community would not be leveled.

The morning brought varied news. Some had been spared. But as the reports of yet more loss of home, pets and livelihood trickled in, I sank deeper into a place of suspended existence, filled with nothing but a numbness that softened the sorrow that was too intense to allow to the surface.

I fought back tears and swallowed hard to hold myself together. I couldn't grieve yet. It was too soon. This was only one of many times reality would grip me by the throat and try to render me inconsolable.

Lesson #8: no amount of personal discovery, therapy or self-help techniques hold you unharmed when the world burns.

The smoke followed as a caustic reminder that all I left behind was still under attack. I couldn't go outside, feel the sun on my skin, find a breath of fresh air or hear the sound of birds anywhere. I was trapped indoors, the stench of acrid smoke bitter in my mouth. The days became a series of ordinary tasks—shopping for essentials, preparing food, taking a shower; all now a privilege that no longer could be taken for granted. The knowledge that over 40,000 people, like me, were evacuated and some did not enjoy such luxuries as running water, electricity and fresh food weighed on me. I felt the need to help, to reach out a strong hand to lift them up, but I was standing knee deep in the mire of my own situation unable to do so.

We moved farther west to the Russian River in hopes that the air would be clean. I found a small motel, one of a few with an available room. I was concerned I'd be turned away because of my dog, but the owner—a dark East Indian man with large, gentle eyes and a broad smile—bent the rules when he asked where I was from and learned I had been evacuated. I felt the kindness and compassion of a close friend emanate from him, even though we had just met. He gave me the best room he had overlooking the river with a private deck.

I immediately felt my heart relax and my soul begin to heal as I carried my bag up the stairs and heard the sound of birds for the first time in a week. As I led my dog to the room, the owner called to me and asked where I was planning to have dinner. I told him I had not thought that far ahead yet, to which he reassured me not to worry. He was fixing Indian food for a friend who was joining his family for dinner and he would bring us a plate. I was overwhelmed with gratitude. Tears welled up that had been waiting to be released and I thanked him from the bottom of my heart.

Sitting on the deck overlooking the river as the sun set, I realized I had been humbled at the feet of this fire. It had consumed my life and caused me to live each moment differently. Within the powerlessness, I found a peaceful resolve. I no longer struggled to control the uncontrollable and I learned to let go, at least for a time. My innate and ever-present determination to plan, orchestrate and manifest my own destiny had met its match.

I was defeated and enlightened at the same time. I was at peace with the temporary and found a sense of deep comfort in the simple, moment to moment joys that interspersed themselves within this tragedy. I found myself being more honest in my emotions, saying I love you far more often, looking into a stranger's eyes and asking with a genuine concern how they were. I accepted charity gratefully and without the defense of pride.

Lesson # 9: everything that happens, no matter how difficult, brings with it something of value. If I pay attention and allow it, I will be changed, perhaps for the better.

Once the fire was contained, I waited day by day, for word that power had been restored to the area where I live in the Glen Ellen foothills. I dreaded the scene to which I would return. Our house was built at the edge of a park where I hiked nearly every morning, immersed in the splendor of a wild and natural place. I knew what I'd find there would be nothing like what I'd left behind.

Once notified it was safe to repopulate, I retraced my journey back through miles of scorched black earth; past the shells of burned vehicles, houses fully disintegrated with nothing but their chimneys intact, past the street where I grew up and finally past the hills where I hiked for decades, now decimated and barren. I finally let the tears flow. Gone were the deer and the geese that wintered over on the reservoir a mile from my house—there were no birds, no sign of life anywhere, only singed live oak and the stench of ash.

I found my house still standing, a pink ribbon dangling from my address post, a sign that it had been inspected and found habitable. It was indeed. But it now stood in a small neighborhood oasis surrounded by char and devastation that stretched for miles in all directions.

My house was saved, but my home burned.

I would recover, as would the community and the

wilderness I cherished, but it would take time, love and acceptance. But now I was better prepared to endure what was to come, having been made stronger and more resilient by what had been.

The Wonder
of the Ordinary

Beautiful Bones
Toti O'Brien

Her head motions catch my eye through the rear mirror. Graceful, lively, and swift, like the flight of birds, the twirls of hula dancers. She sits on the passenger side of the car behind mine, and I should pay attention to the street, but I can't. Instead, I keep watching her.

An old woman. Although her features are blurred (my windows need cleaning), I can tell by the jutting of her bones—forehead, jaw, cheeks, and chin. Straight thin nose, deep set orbits. The hair is grayish and pulled back, but for sure she has beautiful bones. Still, the way her head sways (during an animated talk with the driver) is what awes me the most.

A man is at the wheel. At a glance I make out the pale halo of his hair and beard. He is watching the road, though we are stopped at the light. His shape, steady, betrays concentration. Maybe he is lost in his mind while her head keeps dancing.

Not just hula. I perceive different rhythms, a whole mosaic of accents, tensions, releases. Curves like questions that languorous pauses hyperbolize. Lullabying swings, hesitations punctuated by delicate nods. Extroverted, excited hops and jumps interrupting deep, grave, solemn waves.

Why is the sight so enchanting I can't look away? Beauty in motion, perhaps, or the mystery of youth eternal, undaunted, rising from core to skin. Through the mirror it reaches me full force.

§

A week later, I see another old lady. I am driving—once more stopped at the light—and she is on the sidewalk. She bends over, intent, focused on something. Does she have a small dog on a leash? I can't see it. Is she gathering flowers? On the concrete?

As I watch, her dress strikes me: long and flowing, pristinely ironed. A nice cut, a bright color … is it apricot, peach, salmon pink? A nuance I can't truly name—a color of flesh but decanted, purified.

How daring of her to pick this spring shade, light and sweet, no matter how many springs she has gone through! Not enough to make her wilt, apparently, as she didn't lose her taste for things fresh—first sunrays, dew pearling the surface of leaves—things small, growing, things vulnerable. After all, she might have seen a flower. She bends slowly.

The peach-colored dress is made of light cotton. Flaring skirt, loose blouse, pretty collar. As she pulled it out of the closet, earlier on, she must have handled it carefully, her knotted fingers taking time with buttons and buttonholes. But time matters no more.

As her hand reaches the sidewalk, the light strikes a curl

of her silver hair. Her face is also luminous, serene. Maybe getting old is not all that hard. It depends on how you select your wardrobe.

§

I remember the other one, then. The ancient memory of yet another woman takes hold of me. Was she ancient as well? Not just old? She had a scent of another era, other world.

I saw her on a small, non-touristic Mediterranean seashore. It was dawn, and I was there with my child. Near by, a man sat on his own—quiet, discrete, newspaper in hand. Four of us on a lonely beach and no need for introductions. Nature, silence, and beauty cradled us in a bubble of safe, peaceful intimacy.

The sun hadn't yet risen but already colored the sky. The old woman was naked. She had bathed. She must have been very strong if she could bathe in cold water. Well-being showed on her skin.

How superb was her bare body in the tender glare! The flesh labored, molded, twisted, bitten by the years—a geography of sewn-up scars, mended wounds, tiny bundles of fatigue and pain. But meticulously stitched, deftly embroidered, like a delicate tapestry.

Her nude, haloed by the rising light, was gorgeous. She sat then, her hand playing with the sand, fingers tracing lines. Was she a fairy? One of the Fates? An image of destiny as it looks when we aren't scared of watching.

Ode to an Expressway Egret

Marcy Darin

My commute is like giving birth: I accept it because there is no way out but through the pain.

Only eighteen miles long, my drive home is still cringe-worthy, forcing my humble Nissan Versa to change lanes several times to avoid being swept toward Wisconsin. I hold my breath and pray. There are shoppers pouring out of IKEA and office workers heading home from major corporate headquarters along the Eisenhower Expressway, the major artery that connects Chicago's Loop with western suburbs. Nearly every day, there are crashes—some are fender benders, some far more grave. The way home is littered with cars bearing smashed bumpers and side-view mirrors hanging by a cord. I myself totaled a Toyota when, distracted by a text message from my daughter, I rear-ended a slow-moving Ford Focus. (My daughter would not be teaching her fourth-grade classes that day after what was almost certainly a prank caller threatening to plant a bomb in her Detroit school.) My daughter is always at the top of my worry list, but my mind often swerves from one potential tragedy to another. The sight of red flashing lights on police cars triggers thoughts of heart-wrenching stories I heard on National Public Radio about migrant families at the border, mothers and babies being swept up and separated by immigration officials. Meanwhile, my Google Maps warns me to brace for a twenty-minute slowdown ahead.

My commute, it would seem, is not for the faint-hearted.

Then last September, I got a reprieve. Just after Exit 4 and before Motel Six, I spied her, a dazzling long-legged beauty wading in a weedy makeshift pond alongside the expressway. Her white feathers were resplendent next to the brown mound of earth left by construction to create an overpass. Distracted by her beauty, I momentarily forgot about my own daughter's safety, about the injustice we were inflicting on desperate families fleeing violence, and the nightmare of global warming that might well obliterate my and all children's chances for life as we know it.

I had no idea if this charming bird was male or female, but I instinctively believed her to be female by the regal way she carried herself, as if she were balancing a book on her plumeless head.

Judging by her graceful S-shaped neck, she was most likely an egret, a species that was somewhat familiar to me. I had glimpsed these lovely birds in the oceanside ponds of coastal Maine and in the prairie-like grasses of the Florida Everglades but never on the side of an expressway. I knew that egrets, like most herons, are loners, so I was not surprised to see her without a companion.

Inspired to consult my *Peterson Field Guide* that evening, I identified my bird as a Great White Egret, distinguished by her long-curved neck and black legs. Probing deeper, I discovered that egrets have been associated with well-being since ancient times. In Egypt, an egret was revered as a creature bearing light. The Chinese imbued these graceful birds with the qualities of patience, purity, and long life. For some Native Americans, egrets symbolized good luck.

Fortunately for us bird lovers, egrets have experienced their own good luck. Highly prized for their white plumage that adorned women's hats in the late nineteenth century, these birds were hunted to the brink of extinction until conservationists and outraged citizens intervened. It was no accident that these endangered creatures became the symbol of the Audubon Society.

Would my egret sighting foretell my own newfound fortune?

Mind you, I am a newbie when it comes to birding, although I was lucky enough to spot a rare whooping crane last fall, shortly after I spied my egret. On the wet, grassy plain of an Indiana nature preserve, I was witness to a party of eight thousand migrating Sandhill cranes, their brown-tinged wings lifted in celebration as they danced and hopped with fellow travelers. Suddenly, a nature guide in a green slicker was yelling "Whooper! It's a whooper!" Veteran birders bounded toward an open scope, as did I. Toward the edge of the Sandhills stood a bird taller and whiter than the others. The interloper lingered awkwardly for about ten minutes and then, sensing she was shunned, flew off, perhaps to find more hospitable birds. I was told that some birders wait an entire lifetime to spot a whooper, which number only four hundred in the wild. Was it my egret that brought me this luck?

For the entire month of September and into October, my egret was a welcome fixture on my drive home. During the five or six seconds this graceful wader was in my sight, her stance never wavered. Like a ballerina, she balanced gracefully on her long legs and stared straight at her audience—me. I didn't mind bumper to bumper traffic since it gave me a few more seconds to soak in her beauty, her milky white feathers, and her elongated, curved neck. Where did she come from, and why was she here? She seemed to be waiting for me.

If I had a stressful day at the office cranking out grants under a deadline, I always looked forward to catching a glimpse of my expressway egret. She calmed me. She made me think that all would be well. That my kids would find good jobs and kind partners. That I might find the stamina to hang on to my demanding job until retirement. On those few days when I didn't see her, I worried. Was she swooped up by a red-tailed hawk roosting in a nearby forest preserve? Did she grow tired of the relentless traffic and seek shelter elsewhere? By mid-October I noticed that ducks had taken up residence in the same pond, trampling on my egret's exclusive squatter's rights. When I did not see her for an entire week, I knew she was gone, most likely in search of warm southern skies. I wished her a safe and uneventful flight.

Later that same year, long after my egret had gone, I had an incredible streak of good fortune. Emboldened by a glass of Pinot Grigio at my company's gala, I bought a single one hundred-dollar raffle ticket and won a cruise to Alaska. After forty years of no contact between us, a funny, kind-hearted man I had dated in college found me through Facebook. We are now figuring out how to nurture our New York City-Chicago long distance relationship, including when to schedule our Alaska trip next summer.

Even though her wading pool is now dried up and overgrown with grass, I hope, against all odds, that I will again catch sight of my beloved egret. And so just before Exit 4 on my commute home, I make a habit of checking to see if she might be holding court, my feathered queen of the expressway.

Even though I no longer see her physical form, the memory of her presence remains a balm for my commute. The words of the poet Wendell Berry come to mind:

> When despair for the world grows in me
> and I wake in the night at the least sound
> in fear of what my life and my children's lives
> may be,
> I go and lie down where the wood drake

rests in his beauty on the water, and the great
heron feeds.
I come into the peace of wild things.

It happened to me, for one glorious fall when an expressway
egret kept me company on my commute.

Two but Not Two

Laura Valdez-Pagliaro

for // Sean

Instead of closing emails with a conventional salutation, I sign off with double forward slashes and my name. I adopted this habit from my colleague Sean, with whom I once shared, for too brief a time, a small, square office with a wall-length picture window framing rolling greens of a nearby country club, and under which raindrop-speckled books leaned into stacks of graded essays left behind by students eager to move on. Our teaching schedules rarely allowed us to hold the same office hours except at the start or end of semesters when industrious or panicked students lined shoulder-to-shoulder along a narrow hallway outside our door. In between meetings, we sat back-to-back prepping or grading in easy quiet.

Sharing an office with a lush view with one of the most deeply intelligent and thoughtful people I ever met felt less like a privilege I had earned as newly hired faculty and more like the luckiest draw I could ask for. Sitting parallel a few feet from Sean was elevating and intimidating. It was also a master class on listening. Sean was a supreme listener. He took in what I said or asked with consideration, his replies following an inscrutable, slightly discomfiting silence. Sean brought the same penetrating listening to department meetings, pausing discernably before responding succinctly, illuminatingly, generously. The best of mentors, though I doubt he saw himself as mine, Sean left some things up to me to figure out, like when I asked him why // Sean. In his characteristic way of pointing to answers with few words he raised his shoulders slightly. Just // Sean? *Really?*

I can't remember if I took up Sean's signature before a defeating cough stopped him from taking my last call. The lingering regret over not reaching out to him and his wife, Roxanne, sooner and more often eases somewhat remembering the grace in Roxanne's gratitude and reassurances. Yes, she said, Sean knew it was me calling. Yes, and thank you, she repeated hurriedly. Before setting the phone down, I paused, heartbroken, listening closely to the interminable silence.

Attentive listening has not come easily to me but adopting Sean's signature has been the surest way to keep him present. So has searching for some meaning in the double slashes, since Sean handed my question about its significance back over to me. Visually, the two lines mirror our office posture, inclusive of the narrow strip that separated us. That's comforting. Symbolically, double vertical slashes indicate a parallel relationship between two objects, like the opposite sides of our square office. I like that, too. The rising slope of the slashes forming a forward leaning gap is open to more consideration, but what it all comes down to is me not letting Sean go.

Clinging to particular habits of those we no longer share a common space with is one way to manage the loss. When my friend Murray died unexpectedly, I strained to hear his Zimbabwean/South African pronunciation of *really*. I Googled accents and went to YouTube in search of his soft baritone, regretting all the while that I hadn't made an effort to hear it from him. I can't say or write *really* without thinking of him and Catherine, his wife, also a friend, and their two children who are about the same age as mine. *Really* reminds me to reach out to people who matter to me while I can, and for that I'm grateful. But reaching out and staying connected, like listening carefully, does not come as readily as saying *really* or typing //. It takes me conscious thought, a deliberate effort that I can't manage to sustain. Sometimes meaningful connections happen serendipitously, and when they do, I think of Martin and Elaine Solomon.

My closeness to the Solomons was unlikely. I was a twenty-something sales associate at a Long Island department store working through grad school. They were a couple with three grown children and four grandchildren shopping on the first day the winter sale broke, one of the most chaotic, dreadful days of the year. On a quiet Sunday afternoon, they strolled into my department again and were taken aback when I greeted them familiarly, as if I had been missing them. Unexpected as it was, a comfortable, effortless connection between us was palpable. Over

Martin's signature martinis on a Christmas Eve several years later, we marveled at the rare kinship we shared. Martin called our chemistry magic, and Elaine called me family. Martin and Elaine's embrace was precious validation of my worthiness of love because theirs for me came from nowhere that made any obvious sense. Elaine died on Christmas Eve the next year. Martin followed her a few years later.

As with Sean and Murray, I spent relatively little time with Martin and Elaine, but they remain present in tangible ways through a symbol, a word, and a story respectively, each allowing me to stay connected to them. Surprisingly, a book I read aloud with my sons speaks to a relatable sense of connectedness after loss. Sara Pennypaker's *Pax* is about Peter, a boy on a quest to reunite with a fox he adopted as a pup and unwillingly abandoned. It is also about the fox, Pax, making his way back to Peter. The narrative alternates from the perspectives of the boy and the fox. Along his journey, Peter meets Vola who, in addition to helping him heal from a fracture he suffered, introduces him to the Buddhist concept of "nonduality." Vola explains nonduality as "oneness" between two things that are separate. "There are no separations," she reassures Peter, but rather a paradox summed up as "two but not two." Eventually, Peter comes to understand his connectedness to the fox as transcendent of the space between. It is a parallel transcendence Pax also senses. I find that comforting and familiar.

My father had a particular way of closing my brown paper lunch bag. He would stand the bag upright and align the top edges squarely together. Then he'd take the right corner and line it with the opposite side edge. He'd crease the side, creating a crisp, neat right triangle. He'd then lower the top tip of the triangle just under the base of the triangle. Tuck the tip under the flap. Curl his fingertips into the fold and hand it to me. I would curl mine where his were and hold on.

Gull Woman

Celeste Snowber

The seagulls are back. Or more accurately, I am back. The front of my body beholds their wings. My eyes gaze on their sweep and glide: how they dance and traverse the sky—the sky that is constantly changing. I was raised with seagulls. As an only child who lived by the sea, the Atlantic gulls were my first companions. The seagulls awakened me to light's promise, and I felt secure in the midst of any troubles in my own childhood. I am a daughter of an artist mother, who survived the Armenian Genocide. She was full of love and trauma; both resided in her bones. My mother's screams of rage were present along with the cries of gulls. She loved the sea and made sure she settled our little family in an island town. The gulls lulled both my mother and I to another place.

I never stopped longing for the gulls as I raised my own children far from the Atlantic, near the Pacific. Here, my three sons and I were in the embrace of tall cedars; green fertile growth was closer than the expanse of sky and sea.

I now live in a condo where the large living room window provides a scape of mountains, sky, and a working river: the Fraser in British Columbia, Canada. Tugboats and skytrains accompany the natural world of gulls. I can never get enough of them and am hearkened to memory of how watching them in morning's curriculum is a breakfast unto itself. They perturb some people, but their exclamations are as soothing as anything can be to me. I lapse into deep spaces of comfort and am settled in the haunt of their cries once again. The gulls are not aware of my presence, but their presence remains close to my skin's knowing. The reality that they live within the city's bounds and announce their own particular rhythm bright with adagios restores my courage to show up and dance into my day amidst my responsibilities: multiple meetings, relentless logistics, and small decisions, all of which affect others. It is life of a university professor. But the life, which deeply animates my body and spirit, resides in what calls forth from the sea. I am an ocean child, raised on a small peninsula in Nahant, Massachusetts, outside Boston, and the sea in its many forms is where I claim my roots.

I may have been an ocean child, and still am, but I am now a gull woman. I want to glide as the gulls do—effortlessly. I know what it means to live with effort—a lot of it. Being a single parent for many years, raising an amazing tribe of three sons was a marathon. I might have been taking them to hockey, baseball, lacrosse, acting rehearsals, voice lessons, and multiple pick ups and drops offs of an encyclopedic variety, but the real marathon was to stay true to the track and show up. Show up with all of who I really am—bringing both my decisive and wild nature, artistic and methodical ways, while making dinners and providing an income. I always hoped I could do this with the effortlessness I had when dancing, but instead tears came effortlessly. There were also times of laughter and joy; all contributed to the flow of life. Now looking back, I see there were always moments of ease. I was a part-time seagull in a full-time life with boy birds!

Almost every day for the last few decades I walked a beautiful inlet that hugged the end of the Burrard Inlet outside Vancouver in my home of Port Moody. These walks eventually transformed into the material for my work as a site-specific dancer. Here there was always a colony of seagulls, along with eagles, heron, and changing light. This was my food staple, a physical place on the land, which consistently sustained my soul. The seagulls were lifetime companions to each other and to me.

I am a gull woman. I never saw it this way until now as I am back with the view of seagulls of my childhood. I sit on my comfy chair, and I gaze out at the vista, and they glide by, unannounced, one by one, sporadically. I am lifted out of the details of my work at the computer, and I am called to glide. I am called to soar. Every moment has both pain and beauty. As I sit here, there is unyielding trouble on the earth—and yet the seagulls stay faithful to their true being.

They *play* in the sky.

And I am beckoned once again to play into the moment of coming home to my true nature. A reminder that playfulness is at the heart of creating and living. An invitation to traverse the day with grace.

Fore or Aft?

Wes Choc

All good-byes had been surrendered back at port three days ago.

It was 1966.

The hulking ship, a huge beast of greenish gray, lurked silently in the harbor amid randomly exhaled "bwaaaps" and metallic clanks and groans. Floating, going nowhere perhaps, but unanchored, no longer attached to docks by umbilical cords, loading planks, or gangways.

Around where we lingered, close-by reverberations were more muffled inside this new nautical cavity, a cylindrical cavern we were learning to call home. We didn't whisper, but others' voices were still inaudible ten feet away within these humming hollows. Tucked away in narrow closeted corridors, green metal pipes decorated boxed mechanisms. We speculated about what all these unfamiliar devices did. No one knew, of course, but theories broke the silence. Time passed, pausing only for the next deep-throated "bwaaap" to interrupt.

Some of us lay prone in tight bunks, thinking; some of us leaned against the plumbing. It was private time for us isolated inside our sterile quarters. This was where we waited until the "what next's" materialized.

Duffle bags had been unpacked, stowed. An hour ago, stomachs were crammed full of meat and potatoes from endless supplies of slathered pork chops and greasy fried chicken. We were getting used to funny sounds banging above heads or echoing underfoot. Those who had sought onboard places to go had sated their curiosities for the day. Time wasn't particularly precious at the moment. Besides, the more interesting places aboard ship still remaining were off-limits to us, enlisted Marines.

Lolling around San Diego harbor seemed pointless, yet there was no overt eagerness to depart beyond a "let's-just-get-going" attitude that abounded among us, a craving we could do little to satisfy.

Reticence was the norm. But when there *was* conversation, most guys milled around jabbering about food, Tijuana escapades just had, or telling bad jokes ... y'know, getting to know each other small talk, the kind that suppresses impatience, the kind that surrounds wondering what the next "next" would be.

We knew there'd be a John Wayne movie in an hour ... *Sands of Iwo Jima*. Right outside was our sister ship, the USS Iwo Jima ... so the film was a must-see. But right this minute, bellies full, it was killing time with no place to go. Again! For the third day in a row.

When it came to understanding war, John Wayne's name often came up along with his dirty-faced image hugging a rifle, his low voice never saying much ... all priming us for ... *some*thing similar! Most of us had no idea of what actually lay ahead, but Marine Corps recruiting posters still summed it all up in our minds ... minds ready for that *some*thing! So, we demurred along with other inevitabilities.

Then it finally happened.

Those powerful, deep, throttled, bass throated horns announcing departure boomed several repeating "bwaaap ... bwaaap ... bwaaap" blasts. It meant the ship was moving, departing San Diego to head west across the Pacific. We all detected less-than-subtle vibrations running up our calves and thighs. Eyes rounded open. There was excitement amid unknowns. Guts tingled. But no one talked about feelings much.

We dawdled around to gain footing, pretending seasickness or exchanging comments about things we'd do tomorrow. A few guys exited our quarters and clumped up at the bottom of the ladder heading up and out to open-air. Eyes agreeing telepathically, the "... let's head up to top deck and see what it looks like outside" intentions were acknowledged by nodding heads and pursed lips without verbal comment.

I was one of the last to leave our bunkroom compartment.

In the narrow hall below the ladder up, bunched-up Marines nudged the guy in front with subdued "C'mon!" whispers or a "Let's keep it movin'!" nudges. Though slow-going, oddly enough there was no shoving or anger or profanity. As boots hit each ladder rung, there was a muffled clank, a pause, then another clank. Eventually, each guy was given his chance to ascend.

When my turn came, I followed suit, pausing each time advancing one more rung. Looking up near the sunlit opening, I could see overcast skies and the legs of a small crowd of Marines. Legs mechanically dissipated to the left or to the right. I finally topped too. Taking in tropical air, I planted my right foot on the actual deck pausing like everyone else had. My head was being pulled right by ... *some*thing ... then left, then right again to see *whatever* I could see. My lungs expanded embracing an already deep breath of humid air.

Dusk was pillowing onto the cloud-laden harbor, but distances were still clear enough in all directions ... clear enough to capture attentions. Four uncertain Marines lingered nearby; two finally turned right heading toward the stern of the ship ... two others toward the bow ... all without a single word uttered I could hear.

The guy right in front of me frowned left, then right, then left again, squinting toward a low-hanging sun—then shouldered his body right and lumbered back toward tail end to face the flashing lights—reflections of the sun on city buildings—glass images now miles behind us.

The silent serenity was churchlike. Warm mugginess panned my cheeks as I pushed glasses back up my nose. I straightened my back and adjusted my utility "cover" (my hat). My own pause was ... peculiar. There were no human sounds ... just water swishes from down below. I detected flapping sounds from above, the Stars and Stripes.

In the four or five seconds all this took, the reality of the moment settled into my chest.

The sun relaxed into the skyline to my left, west, squinting in a hazy orangey yellow ball hanging just below clouds and barely above the horizon. The ship was heading straight into the sunset.

To the right, a collection of tiny bronzed squares of orange and yellow glinted and flickered off faraway windows. Against a now darkening sky, once formidable skyscrapers were retreating above aprons of distant red tail lights below—an imposing urban American panorama now deserting its dominion, but sticking to the retinas of hundreds and hundreds of eyes.

To the left, the clear-cut bloodshot ball kissed the orange horizon silently. The red glow, alluring against blue-green skies and artistically painted clouds, mesmerized its witnesses with a depth of distance far beyond that ocean's edge we could see—a simple yet mysterious horizontal line.

The innards of the USS Vancouver groaned subdued guttural engine whines and whirrs while swooshing water skidded by. We gained speed.

Then it struck me. Though we had indeed departed the United States, it wasn't so much about the voyage itself anymore, nor about any warnings or predictions. After all, for months before this June sunset, we had absorbed the destination, endured vigorous training, and digested the never-ending implications of war. Instead, it was indeed about the fore and the aft, this moment at hand, recognition of human choice.

To turn right held comforts for seeing just what was being surrendered, perhaps a warm embrace of those left behind, remembered tears or memories, coupled with acts of stowing these emotions away, maybe for the last time, wishing for an arm around one's own shoulder to identify a wanted inner touch no one would admit to needing.

To turn left tugged the gut, pulling submitted eyes to the beckoning of myriad unknowns—of the "what-might-be's" through uncharted waters in the brain. Yes, and also requiring that same arm around one's shoulder while standing among others so willing.

The pause remained compelling. As had others, I lingered only a couple seconds to glance right over my shoulder, before turning left and pacing toward the bow to ponder what was yet to come beyond that beckoning red glow.

Untethered

Untethered
Beth C. Rosenberg

I entered my eighty-two-year-old mother's apartment with my own key. Standing in her small living room and looking toward the kitchen, I was struck by all the lights she had left on. Near the couch on the floor was a pile of already-read newspapers and magazines, the blanket she normally used also on the floor in a messy mound. On the buffet was a white bag from Burger King. Under the small wooden dining table by the chair were her size four slippers, as though they were ready to be slipped on or had just been slipped off. At her place on the table was a Tupperware bowl full of canned peaches, covered with saran wrap, a fork by the side. About an arm's length away was plate of brisket, half eaten. On the kitchen counter was my mom's favorite bracelet, taken off, probably, before she last did the dishes.

As I walked further into the apartment, I found the bedroom and the bathroom lights on. All this brightness was typical of my mom's night-owl ways—she came alive after midnight. On the bed were three carefully laid outfits, probably set out by her caretaker and companion the day before. In the bathroom, the toilet hadn't been flushed, and from the bathroom to the living room was a trail of toilet paper which had been torn into small pieces, like breadcrumbs used to find the way back.

This was the first time in a while that I had entered her

apartment. The day before I was at a faculty meeting, the first of the semester, where I felt fresh and happy. My phone rang, and it was my nephew, who had never called me before.

"Hey Jakey, what's up," I said cheerily.

"Aunt Beth, they're looking for you. Grandma died. I'm sorry, I'm not very good at this."

I assured him he was okay, and I hung up the phone, and turned to the nearest person to me.

"My mother just died."

I looked at the phone to see when my mom's companion had tried to contact me—it had only been fifteen minutes since her first attempt. A minute ago fifteen minutes was how long I had to wait for lunch; now, it became an eternity for someone else trying to find me. Time had lost all its reference points, and it would take me months to be able to rely on it as a compass again.

I am the consummate professional, and I hate to show my vulnerabilities at work. A female colleague pulled me out of the room, and we were followed by two other women.

"You can't drive yourself home," one colleague said.

"I'm totally fine," I responded.

Together the three women pleaded with me not to drive the twenty miles home by myself. And in the midst of their words, I remembered my mom. I was supposed to see her the night before and didn't. I was planning to drop by on my way home that afternoon.

"Oh my God, I was supposed to see her last night," I said.

The next thing I knew a colleague was driving me home in my own car, and I was talking to the coroner on the phone. My mom was found around noon that day by her caretaker who, as always, entered the apartment with her own key bearing a Burger King Whopper for lunch. She said that because all the lights were on, she assumed my mom was in the bathroom—it didn't occur to her to look down, until she did. The coroner told me my mom was on floor between the bathroom and the living room, right next to the dining table, curled up as though asleep, with no underwear on.

The first thing a dead body does is release its waste, and there, on the already dirty carpet, was a spot where I was told my mother was found. I walked by this concrete evidence of her death a number of times over the next few days, a reminder of death's ugliest but most real qualities, and each time I heard my mother's voice: "Bethie, give me some dignity. Clean it up." I cleaned it up.

She had died in the early hours of the morning. The coroner needed my permission for a blood test because they feared she had accidently overdosed on her nausea medication. The night before her death, her companion had called me. My mother was feeling weak. They tried to get her to stand to go out, but she couldn't move her right side. Then my mom rested, and in a couple of hours she was okay again. However, my mom kept anti-nausea medication by her side; I never knew why. She would buy multiple bottles over the counter. That day, she had taken two, then half an hour later took two more. When her companion reminded her she had taken them already, my mom got angry and insisted she hadn't. Mom's companion wanted me to call the doctor the next day to make an appointment. I was to see my mom that night, but I was so tired. Instead, I called around ten, but she didn't answer the phone.

Grief is not depression. It is its own emotion that comes and goes, pain that you feel in your body, your cells, muscles, and organs. They say it hits when it wants, a life and mind of its own, like desire or love. When grieving, Jews wear a little torn piece of black cloth fastened with a safety pin. It is supposed to represent the first day of abject grief, when you are so distraught you rend your clothes from your body. I didn't wear one, but the utter appropriateness of the symbolism struck me—grief is beyond the rational, beyond the emotional, and it can only be comprehended by others through some metaphor of its power.

Worse was my guilt. I felt guilt about cancelling my date with my mom the night before she died, but I also hadn't seen her for almost three weeks before, since I had been in NYC for two weeks, and the third week I was so exhausted from summer travel, work, and taking care of my child, I just couldn't make it to her apartment. Then there was the guilt that came in the months following her death—the whole year before I had not spent enough time with her. I talked with my mom every day and tried, though not always succeeded, to stop by once a week. I had just gotten divorced. Her companion was there and always told me what I needed for my mom. Sometimes she would gently suggest I "stop by" to see my mother.

After my mom's death, I noticed for the first time advertisements on television: for a $150.00 we could have gotten a battery of tests for her heart, brain, and arteries; for some amount we could have gotten one of those emergency buttons that she could hang on her neck and use if she needed it (I did buy a cheaper version and couldn't get it to work); many caretaker services (which might have sent someone more aware of her condition); and long-term nursing homes (my mother insisted on living alone in her apartment). Each advertisement made me angry at myself, and I found myself too often murmuring out loud, "I'm sorry."

I kept running through my head what I imagined happened. She was sitting on the toilet, probably having a stroke, heard my 10:00 p.m. phone call, tried to reach the phone, sat on a chair to rest, and then just fell over. How scared and lonely she must have been. We had talked of death before, and she confessed she was afraid. In her last years, she did not believe in God. I had always imagined I would be with her at her last moments. Yes, the phone rang at 10:00 p.m., and she probably knew it was me; she always did. Maybe she gently laid herself down on the floor to wait for me. Did she know she would close her eyes and not open them? How grateful I am that I was not the one to find her.

The weeks and months after her death were spent taking care of financial and personal affairs. Not only did I deal with two geographically distant siblings and make arrangements for her cremation and burial, I had to clean out her apartment. Initially, I brought friends with me because I couldn't bear to be alone, but then I had to finish by myself. I spent a month going through drawers and closets, cleaning out the refrigerator, under the bed, bags filled with papers and photographs, throwing away decades of collected mementos. Objects of my mom's I had lusted after—bone china, Judaica owned by my great grandparents, porcelain figurines of clowns with balloons—seemed now to be just worthless pieces of junk, like the old newspapers collected in the drawers of my grandmother's Chinese chest. There were things my mother had saved from her mother, much of it broken and without meaning: a shattered cedar chest that never got fixed, pamphlets from my grandmother's original appliances, cookbooks from the 1950s, record albums of Jewish music. I thought of my daughter, the art, books, and music I imagined leaving to her, and saw her going through my belongings with the same sense of bewilderment.

I shut down all of my mother's accounts—electricity, television, bank—and as surely as I had helped her set them up all those years ago, they were gone. I mourned for her as I took the remnants of her life apart and put them into separate boxes. The further along I got, the slower I was, feeling her presence in that apartment, avoiding the final moment when I would lock the front door and never return. Eventually, I began to see that this apartment, these things, were not my mother herself.

Strangers offered their help and kindness at times when I needed it most. It was the generosity of strangers that allowed me to see the light beyond my grief. There was the man who lived next to my mother whom I had never met. I am sure he heard my cries as I spent the days clearing out my mom's life. I would leave the front door open to let the sunshine and fresh air in, and the neighbor came to the threshold to tell me what a good woman my mother was. I approached the cable man who was at the apartment complex and asked him if he would take my mom's cable box. He later stopped by the open door to her apartment and asked me if I was okay, and he counseled me to choose just a few objects of my mom's and to give away the rest. I went to synagogue for the first time in years, and strangers literally pulled me toward them, comforting me and assuring me I was not alone. Though at the time I could not see clearly, these moments of goodness pointed toward unknown possibilities.

The early months after my mom's death were the most difficult because the trauma warped my sense of time. Like most writers, I measure my life by books, books written and books read. Like most writers, my library has grown exponentially through the decades. There must be hundreds of books on my shelves I have yet to read. I once calculated how long it would take to read all of them, and there weren't enough years in my life. Reading, like writing, requires one's full presence, of mind and spirit. But after my mother died, I could think only of the past and future—reading became impossible. Yet I kept returning to my books, both because I had to teach them and because I yearned for serenity and peace. I consciously reminded myself of the power of literature, which forced me to empathize with other experiences and to see my pain and comfort in the language I was trying to inhabit. Slowly, I found my way back to the pleasure of art.

After taking care of the business of death, the past comes to mind first, memories recalled in vivid detail, like the sound of my mother's boots on the wooden floor when I was a child or her insistence on buying an L-shaped orange sofa. Thinking of the future did not entail imagining a life without my mother, but a keen awareness of how temporary life is, that time actually does have a stop. We are given only so many moments in life, as Walter Pater tells us. I began to ask myself, how can I best spend those moments given to me?

As time went on I realized even more how it is the present moment that matters most, that to make death (hers or mine) meaningful I needed to be wherever I was consciously, totally, and faithfully. I have found everything—color, sound, touch, taste—is heightened. Though my teenage daughter is not interested in me, more than ever before I listen to her rather than speak, support rather than discourage. My presence in my classroom is tightly focused on what is happening in front of me, and I encourage my students to do the same. I have gained a sense of urgency I only recognize from my younger years when I was poor and unemployed. But urgency pushes me forward, makes me honest with myself. I am not always successful in my attempts to stay in the moment; the past—conversations and disappointments—come to mind (failed marriage, failed promotion bid, failed book), but I eventually remember the quality of my moments (the love of friends, the beauty of Mozart, the transcendence of poetry).

I've become aware that I am no longer tethered to Las Vegas and still wonder at the possibilities this new freedom gives me. For almost twenty-five years I have been a displaced East Coast personality in the Southwest desert. I have started to develop on-line classes. The idea of being able to teach from anywhere entices me, and it was never anything I had considered before my mom died. I made money for this extra on-line effort, and I spent a good part of it on my first ever two-week summer vacation: I rented a car and drove my daughter through Massachusetts, from Boston, to Salem, to Plymouth, to Provincetown, to the

Poconos, to New York City. I drove and walked and thought and thought, and the New England views of blue water and verdant landscapes calmed me. I have missed the East Coast since my move to Las Vegas. It is where I was born and raised and where I feel most myself. There is the possibility of return.

Also, during my terrible period of grief, a man, whom I met in undergraduate school but had never talked to, contacted me through Facebook. I looked familiar to him; did I recognize him? After looking at his pictures I did remember him—tallish, dark, and very mysterious. Though on-line and distant, we have developed a relationship through e-mail and on the phone. We are just friends, but I am grateful that he reached out for reasons he is surely unaware of. At first the contact didn't really register, and then the more we talked the more giddy I became. Learning to live genuinely in the moment has taught me to be myself, a verbal and direct woman who is sometimes afraid of her own voice. I experimented on my old classmate with my new approach—I have been deadly honest about my thoughts, my feelings, my life-lessons, and my power of intellect. More importantly, I had been sad for so long, it was a relief to feel good—attracted to someone (even if in my imagination), having a light and flirtatious exchange. I've named him my Boy-Friend-To-Be (BFTB to my friends), a moniker for future possibility.

BFTB and I are now bartering skills—I help with writing

and, as an expert in natural health and healing, he helps me think of my health. Before my mother died, I had never considered Vegetarianism or Veganism. I am no fanatic, but grief takes its toll on the body. My body, like my soul, was so tired and worn, achy, and off-center, unacceptable feelings that I couldn't seem to change on my own. I am starting a new diet as a start to a new self. I know my heartbeats are finite; I want to act in the clearest, most vital, spirited, and spiritual ways possible.

My mother's death falls around the Jewish high holidays. On this first anniversary, I should have gone to synagogue out of respect for her and all those others I have loved. But it would have made me absolutely too full of sorrow. Instead, I light a yahrzeit candle in her memory. This candle burns in its glass for twenty-four hours; I see the flames clearly from all perspectives. I think of my mom and thank her for my new life, a second opportunity with unlikely yet wonderful possibilities and occasions I never expected.

I give myself fully to this light.

My mother would have liked that.

Acknowledgements

Ms. Jerinic would like to thank Daniel Coyle for asking the question that inspired the book, and Brooke Rigler Adams, Lisa Menegatos, and Margaret Jerinic for their editorial feedback on the Introduction.

Mr. Pihel would like to thank all his teachers who have revealed light in unexpected places. He'd also like to thank Christie Lee and Kathy Skaggs for their feedback on the Introduction.

About the Authors

Alaina Isbouts received her B. A. from the University of Colorado. Her work has been published in *Litro* and *Holl & Lane* magazines. Her first novel, *And Then Everything Changed*, was released in 2017. She lives and writes in Denver, Colorado.

Amanda Nevada DeMel is a born-and-raised New Yorker, though she currently lives in New Jersey. Aside from being a lifelong reader and visual artist, she has been relentlessly writing since she was thirteen years old. Her favorite genre is horror, thanks to her father and much to the confusion of her mother. She especially appreciates media that can simultaneously scare her and make her cry. She loves reptiles, taboo subjects, and challenging convention.

Beth C. Rosenberg is an Associate Professor at the University of Nevada, Las Vegas, where she teaches courses in modernism, women's literature, and non-fiction. She has published two books on *Virginia Woolf, Virginia Woolf and Samuel Johnson: Common Readers* and a co-edited collection *Virginia Woolf and the Essay* as well as essays on Woolf, James Joyce, Caryl Phillips, and Elena Ferrante.

Celeste Snowber, PhD is a dancer, poet, writer and award-winning educator who is a Professor in the Faculty of Education at Simon Fraser University outside Vancouver,

B.C., Canada. Her books include *Embodied Prayer,* *Embodied Inquiry: Writing, living and being through the body*, as well as two collections of poetry. Celeste is a site-specific performance artist and herons, eagles, and seagulls continue to be her companions.

Emily Skelding is a part-time writer and full-on mother of four, ages 4, 7, 16, and 19. Her essays have appeared in *Hip Mama* and *Mockingbird.* She is writing a memoir tracing how her strident ideas about education and parenting unraveled during a decade of teaching and mothering in post-Katrina New Orleans. Her family recently moved from New Orleans to Salem, Oregon. A former middle school teacher, she spills her family's secrets on stage at story slams.

Erik Pihel is the author of *Manhattan* (2015), an epic poem about New York City. He founded Palamedes Publishing, a creator of publishing software (www.ebookmaker.pub, www.responsivebooks.pub), and publisher of both printed and digital books (www.palamedes.pub). He has a PhD in English and a black belt in martial arts, and has been programming software for fifteen years.

Fran Braga Meininger writes personal narrative and the blog The Years Beyond Youth. Her work has been featured online on the international platform *Sixty and Me*, at *Ladies*

Pass It On and *Ruminate* magazines, and as a contributor to KQED Public Radio's program *Perspectives* as well as in print in *Sage Woman* and *Valley of the Moon* magazines, and was included in the Sonoma Valley Museum of Art's exhibit *From Fire, Love Rises*.

Fran has lived in Sonoma Valley for nearly 60 years and now makes her home in Glen Ellen.

Kristin Procter currently lives north of Boston, where she collaborates on events and exhibitions for mother writers and artists. Her recent exhibitions of art and words include: *Maternal Garments*, *Parts*, and *Through the Looking Glass*. Find her on instagram.com/WritingMothersWorkshop.

Laura Valdez-Pagliaro is an English teacher with experience teaching diverse student communities at public and private institutions in the US and abroad, both on-campus and online. Her academic research has focused on contemporary US Literature, in particular Latinx literature and culture; popular culture; writing and pedagogy.

Ligia de Wit is a bilingual writer who aims to balance fantasy and romance, two genres she fell in love with. When not concocting stories, she works at a global leading distributor company as a Business Analyst. Married for more than half her life, she is mother to two wonderful teenagers who have surpassed her in height, but not, she hopes, in wisdom!

As a resident of Mexico City, she felt the impact of the earthquake that rattled the city in 2017 and opted to impart the voice of hope she heard that day. If you liked the story and want to let her know, you can contact her at ligiadewit@gmail.com. She will be very pleased to hear that the story touched someone. You can also contact her at ligiadewit.wordpress.com.

Marcy Darin is the mother of three young adults and is a grant writer for a major nonprofit healthcare system in Chicago. Her nonfiction has appeared in *The New York Times*, *Chicago Tribune*, *Parenting*, *BrainChild* magazine, and *Chicken Soup for the Soul*. Her short stories have been published in *I-71*, *Citron Review*, and in several anthologies by Outrider Press. You can read her blog at marcydarin.com.

Maria Jerinic teaches in the UNLV Honors College where she offers classes in writing, 18th and 19th century British literature, pedagogy and creative nonfiction. She has also served as Editor for Topics for *Victorian Literature and Culture* (Cambridge University Press). Her scholarship and creative nonfiction have appeared in a variety of print and digital publications.

Toti O'Brien is the Italian Accordionist with the Irish Last Name. She was born in Rome then moved to Los Angeles, where she makes a living as a self-employed artist, performing musician and professional dancer. Her work has most recently appeared in *Sheila-Na-Gig, Metafore, Dr. Eckleburg,* and *The Mojave River Review.*

Wes Choc, a native "Southwesterner," joined the U.S. Marine Corps in 1965 and later served in Khe Sanh, Vietnam. He carried radio for his company commander, and was trained as a Vietnamese interpreter among several other "in the bush" assignments. Afterwards he became an executive at AAA for 40 years, most recently in Montana as regional president, and retired to Arizona in 2010 with his wife, Carol. After earning Teaching English as a Foreign Language (TEFL) certification, he taught English as a second language in Ecuador, and continues to tutor new U.S. residents locally. He also volunteers at Tucson's VA Hospital working with disabled veterans. Wes has written three books: *Just Dust: An Improbable Marine's Vietnam Story; Inconspicuous: Walter Rothwell's Undercover Journey During the Cold War;* and *Hectic Treks: Unusual Stuff Encountered While Traipsing Around.* Wes has also contributed to several anthologies.

Recent Publications

- Gill Puckridge, Gillybean in China: The Adventures of a Wandering Sexagenarian, follow Gillybean's childlike response to turning sixty
- Ingrid Arulaid, StepMOMs' Infinite Love, a children's book where the pain of divorce is overcome by magical love
- Carlos Hiraldo, Machu Picchu Me, urban poems growing into mountains
- Erik Pihel, Manhattan, a mini-epic poem about New York City
- Tavius Dyer, Shadow Work, poems that take the reader from darkness to recovery

Classic Ebooks

- A Gathering Darkness: 13 Classic English Ghost Stories
- Tradition Digitized: Ancient Poems in Modern Streams
- Joseph Conrad, Heart of Darkness
- Stephen Crane, The Red Badge of Courage: An Episode of the American Civil War
- James Joyce, Dubliners
- D. H. Lawrence, The Border Line: Soldier Stories by D. H. Lawrence

CPSIA information can be obtained
at www.ICGtesting.com
Printed in the USA
BVHW070425151221
624021BV00013B/1576

9 780999 693001